河北省高等院校本土文化英汉双语系列教程

Beautiful
Hebei

美丽河北

燕赵文化概论
（英汉对照）

下册

总 主 编 ◎ 李正栓

本册主编 ◎ 王密卿　高　霄

副 主 编 ◎ 杨清珍　汪艳萍　魏良帅　王毖婷
　　　　　　张广天　李祯妮　崔伊波　张志新

参编人员 ◎ 杨秀敏　黄月婵　王芳芳　李文玥
　　　　　　陈仕贤　杨　光　全雪娇　李潇逸
　　　　　　诸怡宁　严云霞　李　刚　王洁欣

U0331451

上海交通大学出版社
SHANGHAI JIAO TONG UNIVERSITY PRESS

内容提要

    本教材作为阐述河北省情的双语教材，有助于广大青年学生系统了解河北省的历史传承和风土人情，认识家乡的发展现状，激发学生热爱家乡、报效祖国、服务人民的情感，增强青年学生对家乡的认知度、自豪感、荣誉感和责任感。本教材分上、下两册，包括魅力河北、自然奇观、古城古韵、泥土芬芳、人文胜迹、荣光岁月、百年征程、人杰地灵等八篇内容。本教材可供河北省高等院校各专业开展跨文化课程教学使用。

图书在版编目（CIP）数据

美丽河北. 下册：英汉对照 / 李正栓总主编；王密卿，高霄本册主编. — 上海：上海交通大学出版社，2024.3

    ISBN 978-7-313-28401-3

Ⅰ.①美… Ⅱ.①李… ②王… ③高… Ⅲ.①英语－汉语－对照读物 ②河北－概况 Ⅳ.①H319.4：K

中国国家版本馆CIP数据核字〔2023〕第044401号

美丽河北. 下册：英汉对照

MEILI HEBEI. XIACE: YINGHAN DUIZHAO

总 主 编：李正栓
本册主编：王密卿　高　霄

出版发行：上海交通大学出版社		地　　址：上海市番禺路951号	
邮政编码：200030		电　　话：021-64071208	
印　　制：常熟市文化印刷有限公司		经　　销：全国新华书店	
开　　本：787mm×1092mm　1/16		印　　张：15	
字　　数：315千字			
版　　次：2024年3月第1版		印　　次：2024年3月第1次印刷	
书　　号：ISBN 978-7-313-28401-3			
定　　价：59.00元			

河北省高等院校本土文化英汉双语系列教程
专家指导委员会

主　任

　　李正栓（河北师范大学）

委　员（以姓氏拼音为序）

　　安尚勇（河北地质大学）

　　崔海英（河北科技师范学院）

　　崔　丽（河北科技大学）

　　高　霄（华北电力大学）

　　杜　磊（河北工程大学）

　　贺宇涛（石家庄学院）

　　黄永亮（河北师范大学）

　　李晓红（华北理工大学）

　　梁小栋（河北中医药大学）

　　王浩勇（河北农业大学）

　　王密卿（河北师范大学）

　　汪艳萍（河北水利电力学院）

　　王显志（华北理工大学）

　　谢　捷（衡水学院）

　　叶慧君（河北大学）

　　张　润（河北经贸大学）

　　张广天（保定学院）

前言

　　中国位于亚欧大陆东部，太平洋西岸，陆地总面积约960万平方千米，居世界第三位。在这雄鸡式的广袤版图中，雪峰皑皑，群山巍峨，高原雄壮，盆地辽阔，丘陵起伏，平原坦荡，戈壁浩瀚，沙漠似海，森林如洋，草原葱郁，河川蜿蜒，峡谷幽深，湖泊晶莹，海域蔚蓝，山河壮丽，景观殊异，美不胜收。5 000余年的文明，历史悠长，文化璀璨。

　　河北省拥有约18.8万平方千米的陆地面积，位于中国雄鸡版图的胸膛之处。鸟瞰河北大地，北依燕山，南望黄河，西靠太行，东坦沃野，内守京津、外环渤海，其地形走势与整个中国地形特征一致，西北高、东南低，乃华北中心、京畿要地。深厚的文化积淀，浓郁的民风民俗，让河北大地充满了传奇色彩，一代代河北人演绎着"燕赵多有慷慨悲歌之士"的时代传奇。

　　中国34个省级行政区划中，河北省的版图最具趣味，它拱卫着首都北京，并与直辖市天津毗连，京津冀一体难分。然而，在这两大城市的光芒之下，河北省则又是十分低调的——平淡、平凡，以至于谈到河北省，大部分人的脑海中很难有一个清晰的印象。

　　实际上，河北省，这个中国地貌类型最齐全、自然资源丰富、历史文化深厚的省份，它的精彩之处，出乎人们的意料。

　　从地形地貌来看，河北省是中国地形地貌最丰富的省份，是一幅亘古至今绵延几千年的美丽画卷。平原广袤，沃野良田；山峦竞秀，小溪潺潺；海浪拍岸，河湖静安；高原揽月，森林无边；草原辽阔，大漠孤烟。从高山到草原再到大海，从山地到平原再到湖泊，这里应有尽有。巍峨太行挺起华夏脊梁，华北平原辽阔坦荡，白洋淀荷红苇绿，碣石外洪波涌起……可以说河北省囊括了中国所有的地质地貌，堪称浓缩的"中国国家地理读本"。

　　从历史传承来看，河北省是中华文明起源地之一，文化底蕴厚重。神话传说中的盘古开天地、女娲造人、伏羲创八卦都源于此；发现了大量新、旧石器文化遗存的泥河湾被誉为"人类祖先的东方故乡"；黄帝、炎帝、蚩尤在此逐鹿从征战到融合，开创了华夏5 000余年文明史；大禹划分九州，河北省地属冀州，被誉为希望之地；春秋战国时期，河北省分属燕、赵两国，故而这片土地在后世被称为"燕赵大地"；元、明、清三朝定都北京，河北省成为拱卫京城的畿辅重地；革命战争年代，河北省是重要的对敌战场和革命根据地；西柏坡是中共中央最后一个农村指挥所，1949 年 3 月 23 日，中国共产党从这里赴京开创"建国大业"，被誉为"新中国从这里走来"。

新中国成立之后的河北省，人民自力更生、艰苦奋斗，战胜洪涝、地震、干旱等重大自然灾害，为河北经济社会发展、人民生活富裕奠定了坚实基础。改革开放后，河北人民不断解放思想，大胆开拓创新，取得辉煌成就，燕赵大地焕发出前所未有的生机与活力。

进入到 21 世纪，京津冀协同发展、千年大计雄安新区规划建设、与北京共同举办第 24 届冬奥会这三件大事，更为河北省的发展提供了千载难逢的历史机遇。

回顾光辉历程我们无比自豪，展望光明前景我们信心满怀，在全面建设社会主义现代化国家新征程上，河北人民不忘初心、牢记使命、不懈奋斗、不断开创新时代。

这片土地蕴含的时光如此悠长，让人敬畏！

这片土地的自然景观如此妖娆，让人热爱！

这片土地就是我们的家乡——美丽河北！

"为什么我的眼里常含泪水？因为我对这土地爱得深沉……"

知来处，明事理，爱祖国，爱家乡。我们对家乡的热爱之情不是自发产生的，是基于对家乡的了解和认识不断形成的。习近平总书记在《知之深 爱之切》一书中写道："要热爱自己的家乡，首先要了解家乡。深厚的感情必须以深刻的认识作基础。唯有对家乡知之甚深，才能爱之愈切。"

出于对家乡的热爱之情，也出于作为教育工作者的责任与担当，我们以教育部印发的《高等学校课程思政建设指导纲要》及"三进"教育要求为指导，结合我国高校大学英语教学实际情况，组织河北部分高校教师编写了这套涵盖河北省情的英汉双语教材，取名《美丽河北》，供河北省高等学校学生使用。

省情教育是国情教育的重要基础和组成部分，是国情教育地方化的体现，也是爱国主义教育的重要内容，对于深入开展青年学生思想政治和德育教育工作，将会发挥重要作用。

本教材作为介绍河北省情内容的双语教材，有助于广大青年学生系统了解河北省的历史传承、风土人情，认识家乡的发展现状，激发学生热爱家乡、报效祖国、服务人民的情感，增强青年学生对家乡的认知度、自豪感、荣誉感和责任感。中国共产党第二十次全国代表大会报告中提出科教兴国，再次强调了教育的重要性，党之大计的根本是教育，教育关乎民生、关乎国家的发展。我们编写这套教材也是落实党的二十大要求，将价值塑造、知识传授和能力培养融为一体，通过双语教学的形式，把自信、开放、创新的意识融入学生的灵魂，教育引导他们了解河北、热爱河北、对外宣传河北，激励他们为建设新河北而勤奋学习、建功立业，成为激发大学生热爱家乡、建设家园、报效祖国的动力源泉。

本教材分上、下两册，包括魅力河北、自然奇观、古城古韵、泥土芬芳、人文胜迹、荣光岁月、百年征程、人杰地灵等八篇。在这八篇中，我们编写的内容虽不能面面俱到，但也尽可能做到提纲挈领，以点带面，突出有关河北省情的重要知识内容。

本教材信息量大，为帮助学习者顺利学习，我们采用前半部分英文、后半部分中文的排版模式。在英文部分，每篇起始处设置课前导读，每篇结尾处设置练习题，增加学习者的学习印象。教材最后设有附录，弥补自然奇观、古城古韵、泥土芬芳、人文胜迹、荣光岁月等篇章中未曾提到的大量相关信息。本教材可供河北省高等院校各专业开展跨文化课程教学使用。

非常感谢参与编写工作的各位高校教师，有了他们辛勤的付出与无私的支持，这套教材才能展现在大家面前。谨以此书献给伟大的祖国！献给美丽的河北！献给可爱可敬的教育工作者！

中国文化博大精神，河北文化厚重悠长，然而编者水平有限，错误与不当之处在所难免，敬请读者和专家不吝赐教。

本教材编写委员会
2023 年 4 月

Contents

English Section
Part One The Beauty of Cultural Relics

Part Two The Glorious Tradition of Revolution

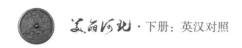

Part Four　Hebei, the Birthplace of Many Outstanding Talents

中文部分
第 1 篇　人文胜迹　文化遗产之美

第2篇　荣光岁月　红色之美

第3篇　百年征程　谱写新时代篇章

第4篇　人杰地灵　河北大地多才俊

English Section

Part One

The Beauty of Cultural Relics

Hebei is one of the birthplaces of Chinese civilization. The ancestors on the land of Hebei have created a splendid culture and left behind valuable and abundant historical and cultural heritage.

Hebei Province has abundant cultural relics, with 963 cultural relic sites under provincial-level or national-level protection, among which 287 sites are national key protected cultural relic units. Hebei boasts four World Cultural Heritage sites, including the Great Wall (Shanhaiguan Pass and Jinshanling Great Wall), Chengde Mountain Resort and its surrounding temples, Eastern Qing Tombs and Western Qing Tombs, and the "Two Spots and One Section" of the Grand Canal (Huajiakou Rammed Earth Fortification in Jingxian County, Hengshui City, Xiejia Dam in Dongguang County, Cangzhou City, and the 94-kilometer Cangzhou—Hengshui—Dezhou Section of the Southern Canal). Moreover, cultural heritage sites such as Wa Huang Palace, Longxing Temple, Cangyan Mountain, Zhaozhou Bridge, and Mancheng Han Tombs, also fully demonstrate the profound culture of Hebei, reflecting its people's diligence and wisdom. Hebei, one of the cradles of Chinese civilization, is distinguishing itself in the new century.

By the end of December 2022, Hebei has 322,610 pieces/sets of movable cultural relics registered on the platform of the national survey of movable cultural relics, and the actual number of movable cultural relics in Hebei has reached 1,402,448 pieces. Among them, there are 60,109 pieces/sets of precious cultural relics, including 1,313 pieces/sets of first-grade cultural relics.

As we approach these treasures, especially the 18 pieces of

national-level treasures, we can truly appreciate the humanistic heritage nurtured and passed down in Hebei and feel the brilliance of Chinese civilization through its profound history.

Lead-in Questions

(1) How many World Cultural Heritage sites are there in Hebei, and what are they?

(2) What are the national-level treasures in Hebei, and which museums house them?

(3) In Division Three, "Ancient Cities, Picturesque Views", a city with the charm of the Tang and Song dynasties is mentioned. After reading this division, please discuss with your partners why this city embodies the charm of the Tang and Song dynasties.

(4) Hebei has an ancient county with four thousand-year-old ancient pagodas. Do you know which county it is? After reading this division, discuss with your partner these four ancient pagodas and their styles.

Hebei Provincial Museum, Shijiazhuang
石家庄 河北省博物院

Chapter 1
The Great Wall in Hebei
—The Magnificence Preserved on the Land

The most representative symbol of human civilization in Hebei is undoubtedly the Great Wall.

Throughout the history of the Great Wall of China, Hebei holds a special position. The Great Wall of almost every dynasty, from the Warring States Period to the Ming Dynasty, has its remains in Hebei, which is rare among the many provinces in China.

The existing Great Wall in Hebei is 2,498.5 kilometers long, passing through 59 counties. Hebei ranks second in terms of its Great Wall resources. The most well-preserved, magnificent, and culturally-rich sections of the Great Wall are all located in Hebei.

Jinshanling Great Wall
金山岭长城

The Shanhaiguan Pass, built within an 8-kilometer stretch between the mountain and the sea, is the representative of the Great Wall pass system of the Ming Dynasty. The Jinnshanling Great Wall is perfectly preserved both in terms of its original architectural components and structure. Zhangjiakou is praised as "the Great Wall Museum of the Past Dynasties", for it boasts the Great Wall remains of many generations, with a wide distribution and a variety of styles. Besides the Great Wall itself, there are abundant historical, ecological, and cultural resources in the areas along the Great Wall in Hebei.

Embracing the sea and winding through the Yanshan Mountains, the Great Wall on the land of Yan-Zhao has witnessed China's history for over 2,000 years. Nowadays, a section of about 2,500 kilometers of the Great Wall remains in Hebei, which zigzags through the ranges of the Yanshan Mountains and the Taihang Mountains: one stretches from the Old Dragon's Head (called "Laolongtou" in Chinese) of the Shanhaiguan Pass on the coast of the Bohai Sea, connecting Qinhuangdao, Tangshan, Chengde, Tianjin, Beijing, Zhangjiakou, and the Great Wall in Shanxi Province from east to west, traversing the northern Yanshan Mountains in the northern part of Hebei; the other stretches from the Mutianyu Pass in Beijing, heading from north to south, passing through Beijing, Zhangjiakou, Baoding, Shijiazhuang, Xingtai, and Wu'an in Handan, spanning the ranges of the Taihang Mountains in western Hebei. Along these two lines lie the most magnificent, well-preserved, and the culturally richest sections of the Great Wall.

According to *Records of the Grand Historian—The Hereditary House of Zhao*, in 369 BC, the state of Zhongshan built a section of the Great Wall. Seeking survival between the powerful Yan State and Zhao State, the Zhongshan State made every effort to protect itself and constructed a wall within the present-day territory of Baoding City, spanning less than 90 kilometers. This is the earliest construction of the Great Wall ever known within Hebei.

During the Spring and Autumn Period and the Warring States Period, the northern states were threatened by the northern nomadic tribes. The unpredictable movements and swift and fierce attacks of the nomadic armies left the Central Plains states defenseless. In response, states such as Yan and Zhao began connecting beacon towers with long walls, hoping to obstruct the horsemen from the north. Out of the need to demarcate boundaries and protect themselves, various states also built walls between themselves.

From the Qin Dynasty to the Ming Dynasty, for over 2,000 years and more than twenty dynasties, the Great Wall had been built on a large scale. In the Beijing-Tianjin-Hebei region, the Great Wall was always constructed along the natural climatic and geographical dividing zone, generally coinciding with the 400-millimeter rainfall line. Behind such a coincidence lies the natural reason, because in this region, to the southern side of the Great Wall is a semi-arid area primarily used for agriculture, with vegetation consisting mostly of forests and grasslands, while to the northern side of the Great Wall the area is dry and primarily used for pastoral production, covered by grasslands and deserts.

Hebei spans both agricultural and pastoral geographical environments. The unique geographical environment rendered Hebei a place where peace and conflicts, prosperity and decline took place in turn between the farming and nomadic peoples. Therefore, the Great Wall had been built meticulously in Hebei, forming the strongest and most brilliant part of the whole Great Wall.

In 221 BC, Qin Shi Huang unified China and, to guard against the southward attack of the northern nomads, he repaired and connected the old walls of Yan, Zhao, and Qin, and constructed a new Great Wall. In 214 BC, the Great Wall (It is called "*Wanli Changcheng*" in Chinese, which literally means "10,000-li Long Wall".), for the first time true to its name, was completed, starting from Longxi in the west and ending at Liaodong in the east. The existing parts of the Great Wall of the Qin Dynasty within Hebei are mostly located in Zhangjiakou and northern Chengde, with a length of over 460 kilometers. Having undergone reconstructions, expansions and the vicissitudes of time, most of the original Great Wall of the Qin Dynasty has disappeared in history.

During the Han Dynasty, when the Hexi Corridor was opened up, a nearly 10,000-kilometer-long Great Wall was completed, which started from Ershicheng of Dayuan (Ershicheng was the capital of a country called Dayuan in the Western Regions during the Han Dynasty, which is Ashgabat in today's Turkmenistan.) in the west, and winded all the way to the northern bank of the Heilongjiang River in the east. Half of the route of the ancient Silk Road followed the course of the Great Wall. The Great Wall of the Han Dynasty passed through Zhangjiakou and Chengde, covering a distance of over 250 kilometers. In Shangyi County of Zhangjiakou, the remains of the Great Wall of the Han Dynasty are still distinguishable. The rammed earth walls undulate with the terrain, and beacon towers stand tall in treacherous locations, silent and solemn, offering a glimpse of the magnificence of the Great Wall of the Han Dynasty.

In 1368 AD, the rulers of the Yuan Dynasty were forced to retreat to the northern grasslands, and the Ming Dynasty was established. The Mongol forces, unwilling to accept the defeat, harbored dreams of another southward attack. In the face of the covetousness of such powerful enemies from the north, in 1421 AD, Zhu Di, Emperor of the Ming Dynasty (with the posthumous title of "Chengzu") relocated the capital from Nanjing to Beijing. In order to ensure long-term stability, the imperial court of Ming

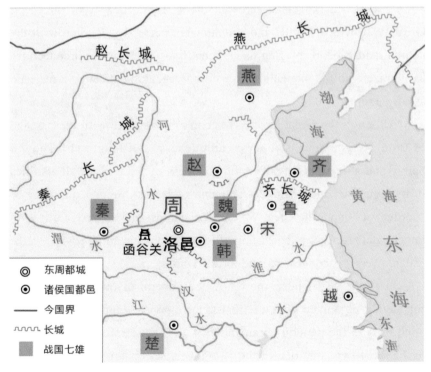

Distribution Map of the Great Wall during the Warring States Period
战国时期长城分布图

began constructing border-defense walls (called "border wall" at that time), which is the Great Wall of the Ming Dynasty.

The Great Wall we see today was mostly built during the Ming Dynasty in the 14th century. Starting from the Jiayuguan Pass in the west and ending at the Yalu River in the east, the Great Wall of the Ming Dynasty is about 6,300 kilometers long, equipped with different levels of military institutions: Dusi, Wei and Suo（都司、卫、所）, etc. It is, compared with the Great Walls built in previous dynasties, the one that had taken the longest time to complete, and the most exquisite one with the largest scale and the highest quality. Lying along the ridges of the northern mountains, it served as the boundary with the Mongols, and the northernmost defense line of the Ming Dynasty.

Ancient Chinese military strategists always followed a defense principle of "setting up fortresses relying on dangerous terrain", in order to defend against a larger enemy force with fewer troops. This principle was perfectly embodied in the site selection of the Great Wall of the Ming Dynasty, as it had taken full advantage of the mountainous terrain. Some fortresses were strategically positioned on mountaintops to block mountain passes, while others were set in deep valleys to seal off vital passages. Such choices unexpectedly created the aesthetic beauty of the Ming Great Wall, with its walls and watchtowers perfectly blending with the natural landscape, displaying magnificent lines. The various architectures harmonize with the mountains, rivers, and vegetation, creating a majestic atmosphere.

Although the Great Wall has become incomplete with the passage of time, its grandeur, steepness, uniqueness, and length still show a heroic and stirring beauty. And the greatness of the Great Wall also lies in its ingenious and creative architectures. In fact, neither the name of "border wall" nor "the Great Wall" can encompass its entirety, for it is an integral defense system consisting of fortifications including passes, walls, watchtowers, beacon towers, and fortified cities.

In 1568, Qi Jiguang, the renowned general of the Ming Dynasty for having organized effective resistance against Japanese pirates, was appointed as the general commander of Ji Town (Ji Town, also known as Jizhou Town, was one of the nine towns set up for military purpose along the Great Wall in the Ming Dynasty), overseeing the over 1,500-*li*-long (or over 750-kilometer-long) Great Wall within its territory. Over the following sixteen years, as the chief architect of the Great Wall, Qi Jiguang made significant modifications and renovations, creating the most exquisite section of the Ming Great Wall. One of Qi Jiguang's innovations was covering the old wall with gray bricks, which enhanced its durability without altering its overall structure. In addition, Qi Jiguang also gave full play to the hollow watchtowers—which had been proven effective in Taizhou, Zhejiang Province—in the construction of the Jinshanling Great Wall. The Jinshanling Great Wall, spanning 10.5 kilometers, features sixty-seven hollow watchtowers, with varying distances between them, ranging from over two hundred meters to less than fifty meters. It has become the section of the Ming Great Wall that has the densest and most diverse hollow watchtowers, forming a rigorous defense system where the soldiers of watchtowers could see and help each other when facing enemies.

Stretching like a colossal dragon, the Ming Great Wall traverses vast deserts, boundless grasslands, and majestic mountains before reaching its east starting point in the eastern part of Hebei known as "Laolongtou" ("Old Dragon's Head"), where it finally dives into the sea.

At the westernmost point of the Liaoxi Corridor, the Bohai Sea and the Jiaoshan Mountain form a natural barrier, with a mere eight-kilometer distance between the mountain and the sea. Since that area near the Shanhaiguan Pass—being only 280 kilometers away from Beijing—had been the strategic passage connecting North China and Northeast China since ancient times, and most regions between North China and Northeast China were plains where the charging cavalry could easily gain the upper hand, the security of this region was crucial for the safety of the capital Beijing. Therefore, in the early Ming Dynasty, Guards and Battalions were set there, and since the middle and late Ming Dynasty, the Shanhaiguan Pass gradually earned the reputation as "The First Pass under Heaven".

Although "the Great Wall" bears the word "wall", it has a more open nature compared with the city walls of other areas. Throughout most of history, the numerous passes along the Great Wall were not meant to obstruct, but rather to facilitate communication and exchange. The Great Wall had indeed served as the frontier for the Central Plains political powers against the surrounding nomads, but during the periods of peace—which had lasted far longer than the periods of war—the passes of the Great Wall became a symbol of order and regulation, functioning as trading gateways between the north and the south, where goods and cultures were exchanged. Alongside the vast stretches of wilderness that accompany the Great Wall, numerous cities emerged and thrived, including Chifeng, Qinhuangdao, Zhangjiakou, Datong, Yulin, Guyuan, Yinchuan, Lanzhou, Wuwei, Zhangye, Jiuquan, Jiayuguan, and Dunhuang. The origin and prosperity of these cities were all indebted to the Great Wall, benefiting from border trade and horse-trading businesses held there. Although the Great Wall was initially constructed for defense purposes, it served as a platform for trade and cultural integration between different ethnic groups in a much broader sense.

Over the course of more than two thousand years, cultural memories have continuously overlaid upon the Great Wall, transforming the cold walls into something warm.

Whether for those who built the Great Wall, guarded it, or even for those who visit it today, the Great Wall has always served as the symbol of the unassailable bottom line of the nation and embodies the strength,

Dajingmen Gate, Zhangjiakou
张家口 大境门

wisdom, and determination of the Chinese people. Although the Great Wall initially appeared as a defensive structure, it holds a deeper symbolic meaning in the eyes of the Chinese people. For a country, formidable fortifications are surely indispensable, but the spirits of solidarity and perseverance of its people are even more crucial, which are also the unique willpower and great strength represented by the Great Wall. Such willpower and strength have once rescued the Chinese nation from dire straits, rallying the entire nation with a determination and a resolute force to achieve survival and success.

Chapter 2
Chengde Mountain Resort and Its Surrounding Temples

—A Testament to Ethnic Unity and Cultural Integration

In the northernmost part of Hebei bordering Inner Mongolia, lies the world's largest artificial forest, known as Saihanba. Over 300 years ago, this area was designated as the Mulan Hunting Ground by Emperor Kangxi of the Qing Dynasty. Every autumn, Emperor Kangxi led his army to hunt alongside the Mongolian nobles, an event known as the Mulan Autumn Hunting. Competitions, rewards, and economic aid were bestowed upon the brave and skilled

The Mountain Resort
避暑山庄 烟雨楼

soldiers who roamed the grasslands. This annual military exercise served not only as a display of martial prowess but also as a grand gathering for the Qing Dynasty to form alliances with the northern ethnic groups. The Mulan Autumn Hunting can be regarded as a strategic move by Emperor Kangxi to consolidate his empire. To ensure the stability of this magnificent stronghold on the frontier, Emperor Kangxi planned a grander system, with Rehe, a strategic location on the route to the Mulan Hunting Ground, coming into his view. Rehe, situated on a key passageway from the Mongolian Plateau to the Central Plains, was approximately 180 kilometers away from Beijing, easily reachable within a day's journey. In Rehe, Emperor Kangxi constructed a summer palace. Heading east, it connected with the Northeast; heading north, it communicated with Mongolia; heading northwest, it reached out to various Mongol and Hui tribes; and heading south, it maintained control over the Central Plains. Therefore, the Mountain Resort and the Eight Outer Temples were built in Rehe, forming a harmonious interplay between them and setting an exemplary model for ethnic unity and cultural integration.

In 1703, Emperor Kangxi began designing and overseeing the construction of the resort. By 1713, the resort was basically completed. After Emperor Yongzheng succeeded to the throne, he changed the name "Rehe" into "Chengde", meaning "inheriting and accepting the virtues and grace of the ancestors". Emperor Qianlong, Yongzheng's successor, further expanded the Mountain Resort by adding palaces and large-scale garden facilities, incorporating scenic elements from southern China into these northern gardens. This created a combination of the beauty of the south and the magnificence of the north, resulting in the "Seventy-Two Scenes" of the Mountain Resort.

The Mountain Resort, with a total area of 5.64 square kilometers, embodies the pinnacle of ancient Chinese garden and architectural art. It is the largest existing classical royal garden in the world. The resort is divided into four main parts: the palace area, the lake area, the grassland area, and the mountain scenic area. From the highest peak in the northwest to the lake and plain in the southeast, the relative altitude difference is 180 meters. Generally, the overall design of the resort demonstrates an air that people from all directions paid respect to the Qing imperial court.

Covering an area of 1 square kilo meters, the palace area is located on the southern shore of the lake and features a flat terrain. It consists of four groups of buildings: the Main Palace, the Songhezhai Palace, the Wanhesongfeng Palace, and the Eastern Palace, serving as the place where successive emperors handled state affairs, held ceremonies, and resided. The Main Palace is the main structure in the palace area, consisting of nine courtyards divided into the "front court" and the "back bedchambers". Its main hall, called "Danbojingcheng", was built with precious nanmu wood (Phoebe zhennan S. Lee) and is therefore also known as the Nanmu Hall. Its architectural style is simple and elegant, yet befitting the solemnity of imperial palaces. The lake area is located north of the palace area and includes a lake area of approximately 4.3 square kilometers, with eight small islands dividing the lake into different areas of varying sizes. The islands scatter in a well-spaced way, creating a picturesque scene with shimmering waves, reminiscent of "the land of fish and rice" south of the Yangtze River. The mountain area is located in the northwest part of the resort and occupies about four-fifths of the entire resort area. Here, the mountains undulate, and gullies crisscross, adorned with numerous halls, pavilions, and temples. The grassland area is situated at the foot of the mountains north of the lake, offering an open and expansive landscape. It includes the Wanshuyuan Garden and the Horse-Testing Park ("Shimadai" in Chinese), characterized by lush green grass and flourishing trees, presenting a vast grassland scenery.

The Mountain Resort, a royal garden, had been designed and built based on the unique terrain and topographic features of the site, fully relying on the natural topography and following the course of nature. It combines the artistic essence of both northern and southern architecture, adopting the style, structure, and engineering techniques of the southern gardens while incorporating the commonly used construction skills from the north, rendering it the exemplar of the combination of southern and northern architecture. In contrast to the magnificent and eye-catching buildings of the Forbidden City in Beijing, with their yellow tiles, red walls, and elaborate gold decorations, the buildings within the resort are not large in scale, with the palaces and walls mostly built with blue bricks, gray tiles, and natural wood, presenting a sense of elegance, solemnity,

Eight Outer Temples
外八庙

simplicity and moderation. The layout of the palaces in the resort is meticulous, with simple architectural style; the scenic areas in the resort have a natural and wild charm, and the palaces blend harmoniously with the natural landscapes, achieving a sense of being close to nature. It is indeed a glorious milestone in the history of Chinese gardens, serving as a masterpiece of the classical Chinese gardens, earning itself the reputation as "the Epitome of China's Topography" and "the Best Exemplar of Classical Chinese Gardens".

During the reign from the Emperor Kangxi to Emperor Qianlong, the Qing court successively constructed twelve magnificent royal temples at the foot of the mountains in the east and north direction of the Mountain Resort. These temples, adorned with gold and jewels, showcased a grand scale and diverse architectural styles. They incorporated the essences of architectural arts from various ethnic groups in China, including the Han, Tibetan, and Mongolian. According to architectural styles, these temples can be categorized into Tibetan-style temples, Han-style temples, and temples that combined the Han and Tibetan styles. They formed a striking contrast to the blue-bricked, gray-tiled, simple and elegant Mountain Resort. This collection of twelve temples is the largest existing royal temple complex in China. Among these twelve temples, eight are located in the mountainous areas in the northern and northeast direction of the resort. From the west to the east, they are: the Hall of Arhats, the Guang'an Temple (now destroyed), the Shuxiang Temple, the Putuo Zongcheng Temple, the Xumi Fushou Temple, the Puning Temple, the Puyou Temple, and the Guangyuan Temple. To the east of the Mountain Resort, on the east bank of the Wulie River, there are four temples arranged from the north to the south: the Anyuan Temple, the Pule Temple, the Puren Temple, and the Pushan Temple (now destroyed). Initially, the Hall of Arhats, the Guang'an Temple, and the Pule Temple were managed by the Imperial Household Department, while the remaining eight temples (actually nine,

The Xumi Fushou Temple
须弥福寿之庙

including the Puyou Temple, which was subordinate to the Puning Temple) were under the administration of the Office of Frontier Affairs (called "Lifan Yuan" in Chinese) of the Qing government. Since all of them were located outside the Gubeikou Pass, they were collectively referred to as the "Eight Outer Temples". Over time, the term "Eight Outer Temples" became synonymous with these twelve temples. The architectural style of these temples is predominantly based on Han-style palace buildings, incorporating architectural features from Mongolian, Tibetan, and Uighur cultures, thus creating a diverse yet unified architectural style for temples in China. These temples primarily served as places of worship for the upper class and nobility of the western and northern ethnic minority groups when they paid homage to the emperors. The "Eight Outer Temples", like shining stars surrounding Chengde Mountain Resort, form a magnificent and concentrated temple complex, reminiscent of clouds surrounding the moon. Chengde Mountain Resort and its surrounding temples had creatively resolved the tough problem of ethnic division in Chinese history, promoting the great integration of the Chinese nation and serving as a testament of ethnic unity and cultural integration. The moving stories happened here about how different ethnic groups helped each other and lived in harmony with each other have passed down through history till now.

🔲 Chapter 3
Eastern Qing Tombs and Western Qing Tombs
—The Final Resting Places of Qing Emperors

During the few thousand years of feudal society, as the supreme rulers of their dynasties, many emperors would begin building their tombs as soon as they ascended the throne. Above the ground, they enjoyed the power of the mortal world, and after death, they believed they could still exist as immortals. For the emperors, their final resting places for their remains were equally important as their living residences, as they believed life after death was equally important as life

Stone Stele Tower of Eastern Qing Tombs
清东陵石碑楼

before death. Therefore, the emperors' funeral arrangements were surely conducted according to the highest criteria of rites of the country.

Thus, imperial tombs, as a special type of architecture, often embodied the superb artistic talents and ingenuity of the Chinese people, housed treasures of human culture, showcased the highest level of planning and design of that era, and concentrated the splendid achievements of architectural technology and art of the time. The Ming and Qing dynasties represent the culmination of tomb construction in ancient China, reaching the pinnacle of its development.

The imperial tombs of the Qing Dynasty were meticulously planned and constructed by emperors. They embody the highest criteria of funeral rituals of China's feudal society, as well as the cosmology, views on life and death, moral principles, and customs of the thousand-year-old feudal society. They also reflect the most advanced planning and architectural art of China at that time. The Qing imperial family have three tomb groups: the Northern Tombs in Shenyang, Liaoning Province; the Eastern Qing Tombs in Zunhua, Tangshan, Hebei Province; and the Western Qing Tombs in Yixian County, Baoding, Hebei Province. The construction of the Eastern Qing Tombs preceded that of the Western Qing Tombs and took 247 years to complete. It is the largest and most complete existing architectural complex of imperial tombs in China, renowned for its grand scale, systematic layout, and well-preserved state.

The Eastern Qing Tombs are located at the southern foot of the main peak of the Changrui Mountain, in the western part of Malanyu, Zunhua City, Hebei Province. The entire tomb area covers an area of 78 square kilometers. There are totally 5 royal tomb areas of Qing emperors: Xiaoling (Emperor Shunzhi), Jingling (Emperor Kangxi), Yuling (Emperor Qianlong), Dingling (Emperor Xianfeng), and Huiling (Emperor Tongzhi); 4 tomb areas of empresses; 5 tomb areas of concubines; and 1 tomb area of a princess.

The expert on world cultural heritage from the United Nations once commented on the Eastern Qing Tombs as "the ingenious masterpiece of human creation".

The entire tomb area is characterized by the Changrui Mountain on the north, resembling a screen of embroidered silk, and the Jinxing

Yongfu Temple in the Western Qing Tombs
清西陵永福寺

Mountain on the south, resembling a courtier holding a tablet bowing to the emperor in court. In the middle, there is the Yingbi Mountain, serving as a writing desk that one can lean on. On the east, there is the Yingfeidaoyang Mountain, resembling the Azure Dragon lying down, and on the west, there is the Huanghua Mountain, resembling the White Tiger crouching (Azure Dragon and White Tiger are respectively the gods of the East and the West in traditional Chinese culture). Two rivers, like jade belts, surround the eastern and western sides. The layout of the tombs together with the surrounding mountains creates a broad and spacious environment that is elegant and harmonious, and it is truly a masterpiece of natural beauty.

Xiaoling, which is under the main peak of the Changrui Mountain, serves as the central axis of the Eastern Qing Tombs; the other tomb areas were distributed according to the mountain terrain from the middle to the eastern and western ends, spreading like a fan. The tomb areas were arranged in an orderly manner distinctively according to the hierarchical status of the dead.

All the imperial tomb areas were constructed based on certain rules and rituals, each containing a series of buildings, with an overall layout that "the front part is court, and the back is bedchambers". The aesthetic idea that "not only should the aesthetic of each individual building be taken into consideration, but also the overall effect of the entire tomb complex and its coordination with the surrounding environment should be taken into account" had been incorporated in every tomb area, so each individual tomb area had achieved nearly perfect spatial composition. When viewed from a distance, the palaces, walls, gateways, roads, and bridges present a magnificent and profound sight with golden and green colors, as well as red and white hues. From afar to up close, the scenery changes and transitions, offering a rich and orderly experience that is captivating and harmonious. The Eastern Qing Tombs serve as exemplary works of ancient Chinese imperial tombs, reaching the pinnacle of architectural art in China.

The Eastern Qing Tombs represent the culmination of imperial tombs throughout Chinese history and are the crystallization of the wisdom of the ancient people in China. They comprehensively embody Chinese traditional cultural elements such as *feng shui*, architecture, aesthetics, philosophy, landscape design, funeral and sacrificial rituals, religion, and folk culture, and hold significant historical, artistic, and scientific values.

From Emperor Yongzheng onwards, the Qing Dynasty implemented the practice that "grandparents and grandchildren buried together, while fathers and sons buried separately". Thus, the construction of the Western Qing Tombs began.

The Western Qing Tombs are located at the foot of the Yongning Mountain, 15 kilometers west of Yixian County in Hebei Province. With a perimeter of approximately 100 kilometers and an area of about 800 square kilometers, it has altogether four tombs for the emperors: Tailing (Emperor Yongzheng), Changling (Emperor Jiaqing), Muling (Emperor Daoguang), and Chongling (Emperor Guangxu). There are also three tombs for the empresses, as well as seven tombs for the *Wangyes* (In the Qing Dynasty, *Wangye* usually referred to the emperor's brothers with granted titles), princesses, and concubines.

The Western Qing Tombs are backed by the lush peaks of the Yongning Mountain to the north and bordered by the meandering Yishui River to the south. With ancient towering trees and majestic landscapes, the scenery is awe-inspiring. Since the time of site selection and the construction of the tombs during the reign of Emperor Yongzheng, tens of thousands of pine trees had been planted at the foot of the Yongning Mountain, by the Yishui River, and inside and outside of the tomb areas. Now, there are over 15,000 ancient pine trees here, and more than 200,000 newly-planted pines and cypresses. The Western Qing Tombs, therefore, is a place with clear waters and green hills, full of verdant and luxuriant pines and cypresses, creating a picturesque landscape. The 14 tomb areas are nestled among the largest artificial ancient pine forest in North China, partly hidden and partly visible, creating a magnificent and captivating scenery. In the tomb area, there are over 1,000 palaces and over 100 other ancient buildings as well as ancient statues, which are all grand and magnificent. Every imperial tomb strictly follows the rules and rituals of

Tailing Tomb
泰陵

the Qing Dynasty, as the tombs for emperors, empresses, and Wangyes all have roofs with yellow glazed tiles, while the tombs for concubines, princesses, and *A-ge* (*A-ge* is a Manchu term, usually referring to the sons of emperors) have roofs with green glazed tiles. The different architectures have rendered the Western Qing Tombs a place with various landscapes and styles.

Tailing is the first tomb area of the Western Qing Tombs, located at the foot of the main peak of the Yongning Mountain. It houses the remains of Emperor Yongzheng, his empress Xiaojing, and his imperial noble consort Dunsu. It is of grand scale and complete in its structure. With Tailing as the central tomb area, the other tomb areas are distributed on the east and west sides, following a similar layout as the Eastern Qing Tombs.

Changling, located to the west of Tailing, has a similar architectural style and is comparable in scale. Muling and Chongling, on the other hand, are relatively smaller in size.

The Western Qing Tombs represent the highest level of Chinese emperors' tombs. It is also an exquisite artistic masterpiece. Each tomb reflects the historical, architectural, ecological, and *feng shui* cultures of the Qing Dynasty, making it the greatest example of the integration of natural environment and the Chinese tomb architecture.

Chapter 4
The Grand Canal Within Hebei
—The Great Artery for North-South Transport

This is the most significant human engineering project in terms of altering the natural geographical landscape on Earth. It spans over ten latitudes, connecting the Haihe River, the Yellow River, the Huaihe River, the Yangtze River, and the Qiantang River, all of which flow eastward across the vast land of China. The Chinese people devoted their wisdom, courage, and determination on the 3,200-kilometer canal, creating this magnificent wonder based on the conditions of nature.

The Grand Canal Park of the Cangzhou City
沧州市 大运河公园

If the Great Wall could be regarded as a representative of Chinese history in a solid form, then the Grand Canal could be compared to a symbol of Chinese culture in a liquid form. The history of the Grand Canal is greatly intertwined with Chinese civilization. It not only supported the transportation of grains but also facilitated cultural exchanges between the north and the south.

This is an everlasting "epic" of the land, which began to be "written" in the 5th century BC. Along the 6,000-*li*-long Grand Canal, numerous cities have emerged. It has witnessed countless prosperous scenes, and preserves many memories of rise and fall. As the world's oldest, longest-used, and largest artificial canal, it includes not only the well-known Beijing-Hangzhou Grand Canal but also the Zhejiang-East Canal and the Sui and Tang Canal. One-sixth of this great project runs through Hebei Province.

The Grand Canal within Hebei has a total length of over 530 kilometers, passing through cities such as Langfang, Cangzhou, Hengshui, Xingtai, and Handan. It is divided into four sections: the North Canal, the South Canal, the Wei Canal, and the Weihe River.

The winding Grand Canal spans over 530 kilometers in space, and takes more than 1,800 years to construct it.

Starting from the year 204 AD, after Cao Cao established his capital in Yecheng, he built the Bingjing Terrace, the Bronze Sparrow Terrace, and the Golden Tiger Terrace. Since then, Yecheng became the political and economic center of northern China, leaving behind a brilliant era of Jian'an literature and marking the beginning of large-scale canal construction in the north.

In order to unify the northern region and drive away the *Wuhuan* (*Wuhuan*, one of the ancient nomadic tribes in northern China), Cao Cao successively dug five artificial canals: the Baigou Canal, the Licao Canal, the Pinglu Canal, the Quanzhou Canal, and the Xinhe Canal. These canals interconnected the Hutuo River, the Zhangshui River, the ancient Yishui River, and the Lushui River on the North China Plain, forming a vital transportation network for Cao Cao to unify the north.

In the year 608 AD, Emperor Yangguang of the Sui Dynasty mobilized over a million people from various places in Hebei to excavate the Yongji Canal, which starts from Luoyang and goes north all the way to

Beijing, passing Hebei in between.

In the year 1271 AD, Emperor Kublai Khan (with posthumous title "Shizu") of the Yuan Dynasty established his capital in Dadu (present-day Beijing). Since then, Beijing has become China's political center for nearly 1,000 years. In 1276 AD, the troops of Yuan captured Lin'an (present-day Hangzhou)—the capital of the Southern Song Dynasty. At this time, the Grand Canal, which once served as the lifeline for transporting goods and supplying water to Dadu, no longer needed to detour through Luoyang. How to straighten the canal, allowing it to run directly from the prosperous regions south of the Yangtze River to Dadu, now became a new challenge in the face of the rulers of the Yuan Dynasty.

Ultimately, the solution was proposed by Guo Shoujing, a scientist from Xingtai, Hebei. He spent several years conducting topographic surveys, searching for water sources, calculating drops, and drawing a straight-line route for the course change of the Grand Canal. He proposed the overall plan of the Grand Canal's "abandoning the bow-like route and going straight like the bowstring", that is, building a canal in Shandong to connect Hebei and Jiangsu, so as to build up a direct water route from Dadu to Hangzhou (the Beijing-Hangzhou Grand Canal). This plan also incorporated the efforts of another water conservancy expert from Hebei, Ma Zhizhen, a native of Cangzhou, who accompanied Guo Shoujing in surveying the river course and jointly solved this problem.

In the year 1293 AD, after the straightening of the course of the Grand Canal, the entire canal became navigable, and it became a vast water system. Compared to the Grand Canal of the Sui and Tang dynasties, the Beijing-Hangzhou Grand Canal shortened the navigation distance by approximately 900 kilometers. From then on, food, other supplies, and a large number of talents from the south had all been continuously transported to Beijing through this waterway. The flow of goods between the north and south had to pass through Hebei. The political and economic status of cities along the canal in Hebei was elevated. Hebei people could directly engage in trade with the prosperous regions south of the Yangtze River, and they could also proceed northward or southward along the canal, broadening their vision, and then gradually go abroad to the world.

Rivers and cities mostly complement each other, achieving mutual success. Famous cities are often born alongside rivers, and it is hard to imagine a city flourishing without the support of freshwater. The Grand Canal in China has nurtured numerous cities and towns along its banks, and has witnessed these cities' budding, development, and growth.

Zhengkou, Botou, and Cangzhou are three typical cities along the Grand Canal within Hebei. Their histories of development represent the development and evolution of the cities along the Grand Canal.

Cangzhou is one of the most outstanding examples.

With a history of over 1,500 years as a prefecture, Cangzhou is a city that flourished due to the Grand Canal. During the late Song Dynasty and early Yuan Dynasty, the economy along the canal in Cangzhou prospered, and the city was praised as "the Miniature of Yenching" ("Yenching", one of the old names for Beijing). As the mother river of Cangzhou, the Grand Canal flows through eight counties, county-level cities and districts here, spanning 215 kilometers. Along the way, there are numerous historical sites, and the canal is well-preserved, representing the authenticity of the original features of the canal in northern China. Cangzhou also holds the

Identification along the Grand Canal in Zhengkou Town, Gucheng County
故城县郑口镇 大运河沿岸标识

longest stretch of the Beijing-Hangzhou Grand Canal among all the cities it passes through.

On June 22, 2014, the Grand Canal was successfully inscribed on the UNESCO World Cultural Heritage List. The "Two spots and One Section" of the Grand Canal within Hebei, including Huajiakou Rammed Earth Fortification in Jingxian County, Hengshui City, Xiejia Dam in Lianzhen Town, Dongguang County, Cangzhou City, and the 94-kilometer Cangzhou–Hengshui–Dezhou Section of the Southern Canal, were designated as the World Cultural Heritage spots and section, which marked the fourth item listed as the World Cultural Heritage in Hebei.

With the successful application of the Grand Canal for the World Cultural Heritage, the ancient wharves, towns, and villages along the canal are also gradually being excavated. More and more people begin to explore the northern section of the Grand Canal, and the cities along the canal are making great efforts to rediscover the canal's history and culture.

The Grand Canal came into being due to people's need of water transportation. With the development of human industrial civilization, in the 1960s and 1970s, land transportation such as highways and railways rapidly developed, and the once-flourishing shipping along the north-south connecting canal became a memory of the older generation.

However, because the canal's waterway and embankments are still intact, the Grand Canal now is still playing an important role in diverting water, as part of it serves as the Eastern Route of the South-to-North Water Diversion Project.

On April 28, 2022, the control gate of the Southern Canal of the Sinüsi Water Conservancy Hub in Dezhou, Shandong Province, was opened. At the same time, the control gate of the Southern Canal of the Jiuxuanzha Water Conservancy Hub in Jinghai District, Tianjin, was also opened. Therefore, the water from the south through the South-to-North Water Diversion Project joined in this way with the local rivers in Tianjin after travelling through the Southern Canal. Thus, the Beijing-Hangzhou Grand Canal was full-line connected by water for the first time in nearly a century. Water diversion will be the important function of the Grand Canal for a long time in the future, and the Grand Canal, which has thousands of years of history will once again flourish with vitality.

Chapter 5
Ancient Pagodas on the Land of Hebei

Hebei is a province with many ancient pagodas.

The abundance of ancient pagodas in Hebei is closely related to the spread of Buddhism, which began to spread early in history in the province.

During the Wei, Jin, and Northern and Southern Dynasties, Buddhism spread widely in China. During the Northern Dynasties, Buddhist temples and pagodas began to be constructed in Hebei. In the Tang Dynasty, Hebei became an important passage for connecting Chang'an (the capital at that time) with Northeast China, further promoting the prosperity of Buddhism in Hebei. It was during the Song, Liao, and Jin Dynasties that the Buddhist pagodas in Hebei flourished.

According to a survey on ancient pagodas conducted by Hebei in 2013, there are now over 230 extant ancient pagodas in Hebei, ranking among the top five provinces in terms of quantity nationwide. Among them, more than 30 are designated as national key protected cultural relic units. Cities such as Shijiazhuang, Baoding, Handan, Zhangjiakou, and Chengde each have more than 30 ancient pagodas. Hebei boasts a large number of ancient pagodas with high quality and diverse styles, including some rare treasures. This chapter selects five representative ancient pagodas in Hebei, and explores their past and present beauty shining amidst the bricks and stones.

1. The Kaiyuan Temple Pagoda in Dingzhou, Hebei

The Kaiyuan Temple Pagoda, located in Dingzhou, was first built in the year 1001. With a height of 83.7 meters and thirteen stories, it is the tallest existing brick pagoda in China. In 1961, it was designated among the first batch of the national key protected cultural relic units by the State Council.

According to historical records, in the early years of the Northern Song Dynasty, the Buddhist monk Huineng of the Kaiyuan Temple went on a pilgrimage to India for Buddhist scriptures, and came back with the legendary Sarira. In the fourth year of the Xianping Period of the Northern Song Dynasty(1001 AD), Emperor Zhenzong (Zhenzong, the temple name

The Kaiyuan Temple
Pagoda in Dingzhou
定州开元寺塔

of the emperor) ordered to build a pagoda in the Kaiyuan Temple in commemoration of that, and the pagoda was completed in the second year of the Zhihe Period of the Northern Song Dynasty (1055 AD), when the country was under the reign of Emperor Renzong (Renzong, the temple name of the emperor) (Some sources claim it was completed in the fourth year of the Huangyou Period (1052 AD) under the reign of Emperor Renzong). This tall pagoda, which took more than 50 years to build and held significant Buddhist symbolism, quickly acquired a new function due to this war-ridden historical period and its unique geographical location. To defend the country from the northern invasion of the Liao Dynasty, the pagoda was often used as a watchtower in the Song Dynasty.

2. The Jingke Pagoda in Yixian County, Hebei

The 24-meter-high Jingke Pagoda is an octagonal solid brick pagoda with thirteen stories. Its design is ancient and simple, with a lotus-shaped foundation in the bottom and Buddhist relics at its top. The height of each story decreases as the pagoda rises, giving the entire pagoda an elegant and slender appearance. On the eight corners of each story of the pagoda hang aeolian bells, which make clear and pleasant sounds travelling far and wide when wind blows.

Also known as the Shengta Yuan Pagoda, the Jingke Pagoda is located on the Jingke Mountain, 2 kilometers southwest of the county town of the Yixian County in Baoding. It was listed among the sixth batch of the national key protected cultural relic units by the State Council in 2006. As is known to all, "passionate and tragic heroism" has always been the most distinctive cultural characteristic of the Yan-Zhao culture. The

The Jingke Pagoda in Yixian County
易县荆轲塔

hero Jingke is undoubtedly seen as a representative figure who contributed to the formation of this characteristic. The origin of the Jingke Pagoda can be traced back to 227 BC when Jing Ke embarked on his noble mission to assassinate the King of Qin, bidding farewell to Dan, crown prince of the Yan State, and others by the Yishui River. According to historical records, Dan once built houses for Jingke on the Jingke Mountain, and after their final farewell at the riverside of the Yishui River, Jingke's tomb, which contained only Jingke's personal clothes, was also built there. In the third year of the Qiantong Period of the Liao Dynasty (1103 AD), the sacred pagoda (called "Shengta" in Chinese) and the temple (called the Shengta Temple) were built on the tomb of Jing Ke. During the Wanli Period of the Ming Dynasty, the name of the temple was changed from the Shengta Temple to the Shengta Yuan. The pagoda and the temple were rebuilt and renovated successively in the later dynasties.

3. The Lingxiao Pagoda of the Tianning Temple in Zhengding, Hebei

The Lingxiao Pagoda was first built during the Tang Dynasty, with a height of 40.98 meters. It is a nine-storied octagonal pavilion-styled pagoda made of both bricks and wood. The lower three stories are made of bricks, while the upper six stories are wooden. The part of the pagoda made of bricks was renovated during the Song Dynasty, and the upper wooden part was rebuilt during the Jin Dynasty.

The Lingxiao Pagoda of the Tianning Temple in Zhengding
正定天宁寺凌霄塔

The most distinctive feature of the Lingxiao Pagoda is its internal "central pillar" structure, which is the only existing example of such structural design in China. There is a central pillar standing on the fourth level of the pagoda that leads all the way to the top of the pagoda. On each level, there are eight beams extended horizontally from the central pillar. These beams connect the eight corners of the pagoda. In this way, the central pillar, the embracing columns, and the corner bracket sets and beams of each level form a steady and integrated structure, which at the same time bears and distributes the load of the pagoda's top and finial.

It is worth mentioning that Zhengding is the only historical and cultural city in Hebei that preserves four ancient pagodas that are of over 1,000 years' history. The Lingxiao Pagoda of the Tianning Temple serves as one of the "Four Pagodas of Zhengding", along with the Xumi Pagoda of the Kaiyuan Temple, the Chengling Pagoda of the Linji Temple, and the Hua Pagoda of the Guanghui Temple. These four pagodas are still standing there proudly even if 1,000 years have passed. Zhengding is densely-distributed with ancient pagodas, which is a microcosm of the overall distribution of ancient pagodas in Hebei.

4. The Jingzhou Pagoda in Jingxian County, Hebei

The Jingzhou Pagoda is located in Jingxian County, Hengshui City. It was originally named the Shakyamuni Pagoda (or Shijiawen Pagoda),

Xumi Pagoda of Kaiyuan Temple in
Zhengding County, Hebei
正定开元寺须弥塔

Hua Pagoda of Guanghui Temple in
Zhengding County, Hebei
正定广惠寺华塔

Chengling Pagoda of Linji Temple in Zhengding County, Hebei
正定临济寺澄灵塔

Jingzhou Pagoda in Jingxian County
景县景州塔

and is also known as the Kaifu Temple Pagoda. Since today's Jingxian County was the former location of Jingzhou Prefecture in the history, so the pagoda is commonly referred to as Jingzhou Pagoda. The architecture is a masonry-structured, multi-eaved, and pavilion-styled octagonal pagoda with 13 stories; its height is 63.85 meters, and the circumference of its bottom story is 50.5 meters. In 1996, the Jingzhou Pagoda was listed among the fourth batch of the national key protected cultural relic units by the State Council.

5. The Stone Pagoda of the Zhiping Temple in Zanhuang County, Hebei

The Stone Pagoda of Zhiping Temple, also known as the Jiaying Temple Stone Pagoda, is located on the bank of the Jishui River north of the Jiayingsi Village, Zanhuang County. The pagoda is about 12.5 meters high and has an octagonal imitation-wood pavilion-styled structure. It has three stories, and each story has overhanging eaves, with their wing-corners bending slightly upwards, giving the entire pagoda a slender, graceful, and dignified appearance.

The pagoda was listed among the fourth batch of the national key protected cultural relic units by the State Council in 1996, which is attributed to its ancient origin and its imitation-wood structure.

Wooden architecture was the mainstream of ancient Chinese architecture, but due to the vulnerability of wood, few wooden constructions from the Sui and Tang dynasties have survived. The imitation-wood structure of the Stone Pagoda of the Zhiping Temple directly reflects the architectural form of wooden constructions at that time. Its corbel brackets and roof eaves serve as important physical evidences for understanding and imitating the proportions, structures, and form characteristics of the wooden architecture in the Tang Dynasty.

What's more, the stones of the pagoda are exquisitely cut and polished, with various fine carvings, making it a treasure among China's stone-carved Buddhist pagodas. There are 32 stone carvings depicting Buddhist stories on the pagoda, and nearly 100 reliefs of various sizes, including Buddhas, Bodhisattvas, and guardians. Both the Buddhas' cassocks and the Bodhisattvas' long dresses are sculpted with naturally drooping curves, while the guardians are carved with rounded, powerful muscles with clear lines.

The above-mentioned ancient pagodas are only the tip of the iceberg, given all of the resources of ancient pagodas in Hebei. A glimpse into those precious relics enables us to see the profound history and culture of Hebei as we appreciate the architectural beauty of these ancient pagodas.

The Stone Pagoda of the Zhiping Temple in Zanhuang County
赞皇治平寺石塔

Chapter 6
National Treasures on the Land of Hebei

History is not static. In the long river of Hebei's history, there is a surge of unceasing life passion and creative vitality from generations of ancestors.

Cultural relics are not lifeless. These treasures, which have witnessed the vicissitudes of the world, embody the labor, wisdom, and emotions of many unique craftsmen.

Cultural relics can be classified into Precious Cultural Relics and General Cultural Relics based on their level of significance. Precious Cultural Relics can be further classified as First-grade, Second-grade, and Third-grade Cultural Relics. In the past, First-grade Cultural Relics were once divided into two levels, Class A and Class B. When we refer to "national treasures", we typically refer to the First-grade Class A cultural relics.

Hebei boasts 18 pieces national treasures. They were unearthed from 7 ancient sites and tombs. The details are as follows:

Places of Excavation and Numbers of Cultural Relics	Names of the Cultural Relics
The Site of the Zhongshan State of the Warring States Period: 7 Pieces	Bronze Tripod with Iron Feet and Inscription from the Tomb of Cuo, King of the Zhongshan State （中山王厝铁足铜鼎） Bronze Table Stand with Sculptures of Four Dragons and Four Phoenixes Inlaid with Gold and Silver （错金银四龙四凤铜方案座） Tiger-devouring-deer Bronze Screen Stand Inlaid with Gold and Silver （错金银铜虎噬鹿屏座） Bronze Lamp with Fifteen Oil-burning Trays （十五连盏铜灯）

（Continued）

Places of Excavation and Numbers of Cultural Relics	Names of the Cultural Relics
	Bronze Lamp with a Silver-headed Human Figure Sculpture （银首人俑铜灯） Zhongshan Prince Cuo's Bronze Square Kettle with Decorations of Kui Dragons and Inscription （中山王厝夔龙饰铜方壶） Tomb Layout on Bronze Plate Inlaid with Gold and Silver （错金银铜版兆域图）
Mancheng Han Tombs of the Western Han Dynasty: 5 Pieces	Mount Bo Bronze Aroma Burner Inlaid with Gold （错金铜博山炉） Gilded Bronze Changxin Palace Lantern （长信宫灯） Liu Sheng's Jade Burial Suit Sewn with Gold Thread （刘胜金缕玉衣） Dou Wan's Jade Burial Suit Sewn with Gold Thread （窦绾金缕玉衣） White Jade Bi Disc with Openwork-carved Double Dragons （透雕双龙白玉璧）
Liu Chang's Tomb (Liu Chang, Posthumously Known as "Mu"), King of the Regional State of Zhongshan of the Eastern Han Dynasty: 2 Pieces	Jade Screen Openwork Carved with Stories of Chinese Immortals （透雕神仙故事玉座屏） Millet-patterned Green Jade Bi Disc with Its *niu* Decorated with a Dragon and a Chi Holding a Ring Together （龙螭衔环谷纹青玉璧）
The Site of Xiadu, the Capital of the Yan State of the Warring States Period: 1 Piece	Openwork-carved Dragon and Phoenix Bronze Door Knocker （透雕龙凤纹铜铺首）
The Site of a Cellar Storage of the Yuan Dynasty: 1 Piece	Blue and White, Underglaze Red Covered Jar with the Decoration Methods of Kaiguang and Decal （青花釉里红开光贴花盖罐）

（Continued）

Places of Excavation and Numbers of Cultural Relics	Names of the Cultural Relics
The Underground Palace under the Foundation of the Pagoda in Jingzhongyuan Temple of the Northern Song Dynasty: 1 Piece	White-glazed Holy-water Vase with Incised Lotus Pattern and a Dragon-head Spout （白釉刻花龙首净瓶）
The Wandi Ancient Tombs: 1 Piece	He Hongjing's Tombstone with Inscriptions （何弘敬墓志铭）

1. Bronze Tripod with Iron Feet and Inscription from the Tomb of Cuo, King of the Zhongshan State (from the site of the Zhongshan State of the Warring States Period)

The Bronze Tripod was unearthed in 1977 at the western storehouse of Tomb No. 1 of the imperial tombs of the Zhongshan State of the Warring States Period, Pingshan County, Hebei Province. It is 51.5 centimeters tall, has a mouth diameter of 42 centimeters, a belly diameter of 65.8 centimeters, and weighs 60 kilograms. With a bronze body and iron feet, this tripod is the largest vessel ever found cast by both bronze and iron in the Warring States Period. Moreover, the exterior of the tripod is engraved with 77 lines of inscription, totaling 469 characters, making it the bronze ware ever found in the Warring States Period that has the longest inscription.

The inscription on it documents the history of the Zhongshan State and the Warring States Period, making up for the lack of historical documentation on the genealogy of the Kings of the Zhongshan State. It also confirms the accounts of some important historical events in historical texts, making it of great value for historical research. As a result, the tripod was included in the first batch of cultural relics prohibited from leaving China in 2002. It is now housed in Hebei Museum.

Bronze Tripod with Iron Feet and Inscription from the Tomb of Cuo, King of the Zhongshan State
中山王厝铁足铜鼎

2. Bronze Table Stand with Sculptures of Four Dragons and Four Phoenixes Inlaid with Gold and Silver (from the site of the Zhongshan State of the Warring States Period)

The base of the bronze table stand is in the shape of a circular ring, supported by four (two male and two female) kneeling sika deer. The sika deer take on a gentle look, with their limbs curled; they have spots inlaid with gold on their bodies and *yuntou* cloud patterns (*Yuntou* cloud pattern, also known as Ruyi cloud pattern, resembles a drooping Ruyi in shape, and is a typical cloud pattern decoration on many cultural relics.) on their cheeks. The outer wall of the base is adorned with interlinked cloud patterns, creating a clear, elegant, and delicate design that balances tenderness and strength. The base has a concave cambered surface, and the surface is decorated with spiral cloud patterns. On the cambered surface of the base, there are four standing dragons, each has one head and two tails, and they are facing four different directions. The dragons hold up their heads high, and they stand up with their front limbs supporting them and their claws holding onto the base; each of them has two wings on its back. For the two dragons on each side, their bodies face almost opposite directions, while their tails cross, forming the shape of a ring, and their two tails are hooking their horns from the back. The long necks and the chests of the dragons are decorated with scale patterns, the coiled sections of their bodies and the feathers on their wings are adorned with long-feather patterns, and the posterior tail gradually tapers with python-skin patterns. At the intersection of the coiled sections of the adjacent dragons, there are long hooked feather-shaped decorations that form an arch-shaped connection with the central partition. The decorative patterns on the dragons' bodies are free-flowing, natural, and steady, vividly depicting the majestic demeanor and unique charm of the dragons. Between the crossed coiled sections of the bodies of the dragons on each of the four sides

Bronze Table Stand with Sculptures of Four Dragons and Four Phoenixes Inlaid with Gold and Silver
错金银四龙四凤铜方案座

of this stand, there is a phoenix stretching its neck and uttering a cry, with a chaplet on its head, spotted-feather patterns on its neck, long-feather patterns on its wings, and slender and even-longer-feather patterns on its trailing tail, looking lively, gorgeous, elegant, and charming. Each of the four dragons is supporting a *dougong* (*Dougong* is a unique component of Chinese architecture, composed of square blocks, risers, arches, braces, and uplifts, which are respectively called *Dou*, *Sheng*, *Gong*, *Qiao*, and *Ang* in Chinese.), which is of the one-*Dou* and two-*Shengs* style in structure, on its muzzle. The *dougongs* support the square frame on it, and both the *dougongs* and the frame are decorated with interlinked cloud patterns. This stand serves as the earliest example of employing *dougongs* in practice in China. The table stand has a complicated structure with sculptures of lively dragons and phoenixes, and its beautiful patterns inlaid with gold and silver are full of variety but not over-elaborate, vibrant but not disordered, representing the harmony between the form and the content, as well as the general structure and the details. Moreover, it is full of curved structures, and shows uniqueness and diversity, serving as a treasure among handicrafts inlaid with gold and silver. The cultural relic is now housed in Hebei Museum.

3. Tiger-devouring-deer Bronze Screen Stand Inlaid with Gold and Silver (from the site of the Zhongshan State of the Warring States Period)

The bronze screen stand is 51 centimeters in length, 21.9 centimeters in height, and 26.6 kilograms in weight. The tiger sculpture serves as the main part of the screen stand; its eyes are wide-open, with both ears erect, as it is trying to devour a little deer. The deer seems to be struggling

Tiger-devouring-deer Bronze Screen Stand Inlaid with Gold and Silver

错金银铜虎噬鹿屏座

desperately in the tiger's mouth, with its short tail raising in an effort to escape, but it still cannot get away. The tiger's hind legs exert force against the ground, while its front body crouches down, forming a curved shape. The tiger's right front paw is suspended in the air as it grabs the deer, and the balance of the stand is supported by the deer's legs. The overall design of the artifact is ingenious and natural. The patterns on the furs of both the tiger and deer are inlaid with gold and silver, rendering the sculptures of the two animals lively and vivid.

At the neck and buttocks of the tiger, there is a rectangular bracket on each side. The exteriors of the brackets are decorated with goat heads, and the mouths of the goats serve as the brackets' openings. When the two brackets are aligned along a straight line, they form an angle of approximately 84 degrees, close to a right angle, creating a curved shape that perfectly accommodates the screen. The entire artifact showcases the dynamic movements and body structures of the tiger and the deer, enhancing its artistic effect. The design of this artifact is clever, and the craftsmanship is exquisite, making it extremely rare in China. It is now housed in Hebei Museum.

4. Bronze Lamp with Fifteen Oil-burning Trays (from the site of the Zhongshan State of the Warring States Period)

The Bronze Lamp with Fifteen Oil-burning Trays dates back to the Warring States Period. It was unearthed in 1977 from the tomb of Cuo, King of the Zhongshan State, in Sanji Village, Pingshan County. Standing at a height of 82.9 centimeters, it is by far the tallest lamp discovered of the Warring States Period. The overall design resembles a large tree, with the main trunk standing on a hollow-out base adorned with *Kui* dragon patterns. (*Kui* dragon is a mythical creature in the myths and legends of the ancient Chinese culture.) The base is supported by three fierce tigers, and each tiger has one head and two bodies, holding a circular ring in its mouth. There are seven branches extending from the trunk, which together hold the fifteen lamp trays. The lamp trays are arranged in an orderly and artistic manner. Each branch can be disassembled, with unique tenon shapes for easy installation and the option to adjust the number of lamp trays as needed. The branches and the trunk are adorned with a winding *Kui* dragon and some chirping

Bronze Lamp with Fifteen Oil-
burning Trays
十五连盏铜灯

birds and playful monkeys. Two bare-chested servants wearing short lower garments from the *Xianyu* tribe (*Xianyu* was the name of an ancient tribe in China, and they are the ancestors of the people of the Zhongshan State.) are standing under the tree, throwing food to the monkeys in the tree. There are two inscriptions on the base of the lamp, with a total of 24 characters. The Bronze Lamp is now housed in Hebei Museum.

5. Bronze Lamp with a Silver-headed Human Figure Sculpture (from the site of the Zhongshan State of the Warring States Period)

This lamp measures 66.4 centimeters in height and is composed of a bronze silver-headed human figurine, two bronze *Panchi* rods (*Panchi*, also called *Chi*, is a snake-like mythical creature in the dragon category.), and three bronze oil-burning trays. The central part of the lamp structure features a male figure, which is not only the main component but also the focal point of the creative design. The figure stands on a square base adorned with animal patterns, with arms extending horizontally on both sides. His body is fitted with a silver head, featuring thick eyebrows, a short beard, a flat face, high cheekbones, and slightly upturned corners of the mouth. His eyes are inset with black gemstones, shining brightly. The figure is dressed in a tight garment with wide sleeves, and the hem of his lower garment is drooping on the ground, dividing into two parts, revealing both feet at the fork. His attire is decorated with spiral cloud patterns and enhanced with black and vermilion lacquer, showcasing its extraordinary magnificence. The man holds the tail of a *Panchi* in his left hand, while the *Panchi* stretches its body horizontally and holds up its head to support an oil-burning tray. However, there is another *Panchi* winding itself in the base plate, which cranes its neck and bites the first *Panchi* with its mouth. In the right hand of the bronze figure, there is also a *Panchi*, whose mouth holds a supporting rod with dragon patterns that are inlaid with silver. The rod

Bronze Lamp with a Silver-headed Human Figure Sculpture
银首人俑铜灯

is intricately carved with a relief winding *Panchi* and a climbing monkey, depicting a playful scene of a *Panchi* chasing a monkey. At the top of the rod, there is an oil-burning tray, which is the highest point of the lamp. The general structure of the lamp is well-arranged, whose outline seems to form a regular right-angled triangle, and the design that the human figurine controls the *Panchis*, connecting the three oil-burning trays naturally, displays exceptional craftsmanship. The three lamp trays are all hollow and circular with grooves. Each tray has three skewers for supporting the wicks of the oil lamp, and the bases and side walls of the trays expand outward at the skewer locations. With a total of nine skewers across the three dishes, the number "nine" is deliberately arranged, as it symbolizes infinity. The lamp is not only the most richly ornamented lighting equipment with a relatively complicated form ever seen from the Warring States Period, but also a relatively high lamp with the human sculpture from that period. It exemplifies the perfect combination of practicality and decorative artistry. It is now housed in Hebei Museum.

6. Bronze Square Kettle with Decorations of *Kui* Dragons and Inscription from the Tomb of Cuo, King of the Zhongshan State (from the site of the Zhongshan State of the Warring States Period)

The bronze square kettle has a height of 63 centimeters, a maximum diameter of 35 centimeters, and weighs 28.72 kilograms. It is a ceremonial vessel with a unique design. On its four smooth and flat belly walls, elegant seal script characters are delicately engraved with fine strokes. The inscription on the vessel consists of a total of 450 characters. The general meaning of the inscription is that in the fourteenth year of the reign of the King of Zhongshan State, the king ordered his minister Sima Zhou to make this vessel from the bronze ceremonial vessels obtained from the Yan State. The inscription serves as a reminder to his son, the future king of the Zhongshan State, to learn from the lessons of the rebellion of Zizhi, Minister of the Yan State, and emphasizes the loyalty and achievements of Minister

Zhongshan Prince Cuo's Bronze Square Kettle with Decorations of *Kui* Dragons and Inscription
中山王厝夔龙饰铜方壶

Sima Zhou in defeating the Yan State. It also elucidates the principles of how to recruit talented individuals, gain the support of the people, and consolidate political power. It is now housed in Hebei Museum.

7. Tomb Layout on Bronze Plate Inlaid with Gold and Silver (from the site of the Zhongshan State of the Warring States Period)

The tomb layout is a construction plan of the Zhongshan King's tomb area made on a bronze plate. The gold and silver sheets as well as the silver thread were inlaid into the bronze plate, outlining the architectural plan of the king's tomb, the queen's tomb (the king's wife, who died at the same time with the king or died after the king's death), the tomb of the "mourning queen" (the king's former wife, who died before the king's death), and the tombs of two concubines. It is worth mentioning that the directions of the map are opposite to today's conventional way of direction indication, with the top representing the south and the bottom representing the north, while the left representing the east and the right representing the west. The map also includes a clear 1:500 scale and some detailed textual descriptions. There are 24 markings using "*chi*" (a Chinese unit for measurement of length) as the unit of measurement and 14 markings using "*bu*" (a Chinese ancient unit for measurement of length, equivalent to five

Tomb Layout on Bronze Plate Inlaid with Gold and Silver
错金银铜版兆域图

chi), making it the earliest bronze plate architectural plan map with scale ever found in the world. It is now housed in Hebei Museum.

8. Mount Bo Bronze Aroma Burner Inlaid with Gold (from Mancheng Han Tombs of the Western Han Dynasty)

The bronze aroma burner was unearthed in 1968 from the tomb of Liu Sheng (posthumously known as "Jing", the ruler of the Zhongshan State, which is one of the regional states of the Western Han Dynasty) in Mancheng County, Hebei Province. It is a bronze ware used as an aroma burner. It is called the Mount Bo Aroma Burner Inlaid with Gold because its overall design symbolizes the legendary mountain in the sea, the Mount Bo.

Mount Bo Bronze Aroma Burner
Inlaid with Gold
错金铜博山炉

This aroma burner was buried with Liu Sheng, the ruler of the Zhongshan State, who was born by a concubine of Emperor Liu Qi (posthumously known as "Xiaojing"). Liu Sheng has been best-known for his luxurious and dissipated lifestyle, and he had a preference for "top luxury items" in his life. The famous national treasures, the two sets of Jade Burial Suit Sewn with Gold Thread and the Gilded Bronze Changxin Palace Lantern, were also unearthed from his tomb. Therefore, there is no wonder that the aroma burner is referred to as the "most luxurious aroma burner in history". It is exquisitely crafted and exceptionally beautiful. It is now housed in Hebei Museum. It is now housed in Hebei Museum.

9. Gilded Bronze Changxin Palace Lantern (from Mancheng Han Tombs of the Western Han Dynasty)

The palace lantern is a gilded bronze ware from the Western Han Dynasty. It is believed to have been made around 151 BC, so it has a history of over 2,200 years. The lantern was unearthed in 1968 from the tomb of Dou Wan, the wife of Liu Sheng. It is named Changxin Palace Lamp because it bears the inscription "Changxin" on its body.

Gilded Bronze Changxin
Palace Lantern
长信宫灯

10. Liu Sheng's Jade Burial Suit Sewn with Gold Thread (from Mancheng Han Tombs of the Western Han Dynasty)

Liu Sheng's Jade Burial Suit Sewn with Gold Thread was unearthed from the tomb of Liu Sheng in May, 1968 in Mancheng County, Baoding. It is now housed in Hebei Museum.

With a length of 1.88 meters, this jade suit is covered with 2,498 pieces of jade and sewn with 1,100 grams of gold thread. The appearance of the jade suit resembles that of a male figure, with broad shoulders, a protruding abdomen, and sturdy limbs. Under the abdomen, there is a protective cover for the male genitalia. The head features a prominent nose and three narrow slits representing the eyes and mouth. The jade suit consists of six separate parts: the headpiece, the upper garment, the sleeve tubes, the trouser tubes, the gloves, and the shoes. Each part can be detached from one another, resembling a garment that had been cut and sewn by a tailor. The headpiece consists of the coverings for the face and the head, and the upper garment has a front piece and a back piece. The sleeve tubes, trouser tubes, gloves, and shoes are in pairs so that they are designed for the left and the right parts of the body respectively. The jade pieces used in the suit are mostly rectangular or square in shape, although there are also trapezoidal, triangular, quadrilateral, and polygonal

Liu Sheng's Jade Burial Suit Sewn with Gold Thread
刘胜金缕玉衣

pieces. The largest jade pieces measure 4.5 centimeters in length and 3.5 centimeters in width and are used on the bottoms of the feet. The smallest jade pieces are only the size of an adult's thumbnail, which are used to cover the fingers of the dead. Along with the Jade Burial Suit, there are also a gilded jade-inlaid bronze pillow, nine jade plugs for the nine orifices of the body, two jade items for hand-holding, and eighteen jade *bi* discs used for funerary purposes, forming a set of top-standard jade burial items from the Han Dynasty.

11. Dou Wan's Jade Burial Suit Sewn with Gold Thread (from Mancheng Han Tombs of the Western Han Dynasty)

Dou Wan's Jade Burial Suit Sewn with Gold Thread was unearthed from the tomb of Dou Wan, Liu Sheng's wife, in Mancheng County, Baoding City in 1968. The jade suit measures 1.72 meters in length and is made of Xiuyan jade (Xiuyan jade, one of the four famous types of jade in China. It is named after its place of origin, Xiuyan County, Liaoning Province.), with most pieces being pure green in color and some featuring gray-white and yellow-brown shades. The suit is divided into five parts, consisting of a total of 2,160 jade pieces and approximately 700 grams of gold thread. The jade suit is similar to that of Liu Sheng's tomb, and there is also a gilded jade-inlaid bronze pillow positioned beneath her head. It is now housed in Hebei Museum.

Dou Wan's Jade Burial Suit Sewn with Gold Thread
窦绾金缕玉衣

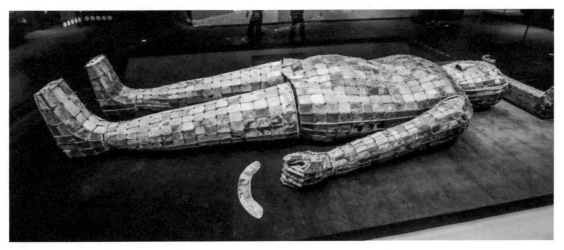

12. White Jade Bi Disc with Openwork-carved Double Dragons (from Mancheng Han Tombs of the Western Han Dynasty)

White Jade Bi Disc with Openwork-carved Double Dragons was unearthed from the tomb of Liu Sheng in Mancheng County, Baoding City in 1968. It is 25.9 centimeters in height, and the diameter for the outer circle of the jade disc is 13.4 centimeters. The jade is crystal clear and pure white, with finely carved millet patterns (Millet pattern is a type of decoration on jade artifacts, first appearing in jade artifacts from the Spring and Autumn Period. The pattern resembles the sprouting leaves of millet and is a product of the development of agricultural civilization, related to the food on which humans depend for survival. It symbolizes the awakening of all things, a vibrant scene, and people's hope for a bountiful agricultural harvest.) on both sides of the disc, and edges raised around the perimeter. At the top of the jade disc, there is a high *niu* (The carved decoration at the top of a jade disc is called a *niu* in Chinese.) with an openwork-carved pattern of double dragons and spiral cloud patterns. The patterns of it are beautiful and vivid, and the carvings are exquisite, making it a treasure among the Han Dynasty jade artifacts. It is now housed in Hebei Museum.

White Jade Bi Disc with Openwork-carved Double Dragons

透雕双龙白玉璧

13. Jade Screen Openwork Carved with Stories of Chinese Immortals (from Liu Chang's tomb (Liu Chang, posthumously known as "Mu"), king of the Regional State of Zhongshan of the Eastern Han Dynasty)

The jade screen openwork was unearthed from the tomb of Liu Chang, King of the Regional State of Zhongshan during the Eastern Han Dynasty, and Dingzhou served as its capital for over 300 years during the Western Han Dynasty and the Eastern Han Dynasty. There were totally 17 generations of rulers during these two periods, and Liu Chang was the 16th generation, specifically the 6th generation of Zhongshan kings during the Eastern Han Dynasty.

This jade screen openwork is composed of four pieces of openwork-carved jade panels. On both sides, there are two pieces of jade panels (The shape of the jade panels on the two sides of the screen is called *Shuang Sheng* in Chinese. "*Shuang Sheng*" refers to the shape of an item formed by two interlocking diamonds or circles. It is a traditional decorative art.) serving as supports, and they are mainly carved with the patterns of the Azure Dragon and the White Tiger (The Azure Dragon, the White Tiger, the Vermilion Bird, and the Black Tortoise are respectively the gods of the East, the West, the North and the South in ancient Chinese mythology, originating from the ancient Chinese people's worship of star deities.).

Jade Screen Openwork Carved with Stories of Chinese Immortals
透雕神仙故事玉座屏

The two panels in the middle have a slightly crescent shape and are inserted into the two panels on both sides with tenons, with openwork carvings of figures, birds, and animals. In the center of the upper piece of the jade screen is the "Queen Mother of the West" (She is called *Xiwangmu* in Chinese. She is the supreme goddess of Taoism.) with a tall headdress, seated by a table, and accompanied by the Vermilion Bird, a fox, and a three-legged crow. (Three-legged crow is one of the divine birds in ancient Chinese myths and legends.) In the center of the lower piece of jade screen is the "King Father of the East" (He is called *Dongwanggong* in Chinese. He is the supreme god of Taoism, and is considered to be the *Yang* deity in *Yin* and *Yang*, corresponding to the *Yin* deity, the Queen Mother of the West.), whose hair is brushed back. He is seated by a table, accompanied by an attendant, a bear, and the Black Tortoise. These decorative patterns vividly reflect the people's worship of the immortals during the Han Dynasty. It is now housed in Dingzhou Museum.

14. Millet-patterned Green Jade Bi Disc with Its *niu* Decorated with a Dragon and a Chi Holding a Ring Together (from Liu Chang's tomb, King of the Regional State of Zhongshan of the Eastern Han Dynasty)

This cultural relic was unearthed from the tomb of Liu Chang of the Eastern Han Dynasty. It is now housed in Dingzhou Museum.

This jade disc has a total height of 30.5 centimeters and is carved from Xinjiang Hetian green jade (Xinjiang Hetian green jade is one of the four categories of Hetian jade, distributed in the Kunlun Mountains within Xinjiang, China. The jade is delicate and gentle, with a deep and pure color, presenting a vigorous spirit, symbolizing a long-lasting foundation.). The jade disc has a semi-translucent quality with a gentle and lustrous surface, while some areas show reddish-brown hues due to natural oxidation. The inner and outer edges of the jade disc feature plain wide bands. At the top of the jade disc, there is a *niu* with the openwork-carved pattern of a dragon and a *Chi* holding a ring together; on both sides of the jade disc, there is an openwork-carved dragon on one side and an openwork-carved *Chi* on the other side. The features of the dragons and *Chis*, such as their mouths, noses, eyes, ears, and feet, are delicately carved with incised lines. The surface of the jade disc is adorned with neatly carved millet patterns. Jade *bi* discs were ceremonial objects used by ancient Chinese people for rituals, symbolizing the connection between heaven and earth. The circular hole in the *bi* was believed to be a pathway to heaven, facilitating people, especially the ruler, to communicate with heaven. In ancient China, grain cultivation was of paramount importance, with millet being one of the earliest crops successfully cultivated by our ancestors. During the Han Dynasty, grain cultivation became the most significant agricultural activity. As food was considered essential for the people, the rulers of the Han Dynasty regarded agriculture as the foundation of the state. In ancient sacrificial ceremonies, agricultural deities were the first to be worshiped, and the inclusion of millet patterns in the decoration of ceremonial objects represented the ruler's desire for abundant harvests and state prosperity. Jade *bi* discs combined the authority of the gods with the authority of the ruler through god-worship rituals, reflecting the belief in the harmony between heaven and mankind during that period. It also showcased the ruler's dedication to "respecting heaven, protecting the people, and promoting virtue" to ensure the eternal prosperity of the state.

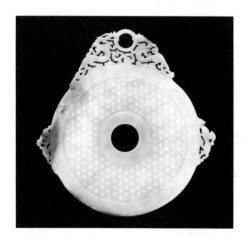

Millet-patterned Green Jade Bi Disc with Its *niu* Decorated with a Dragon and a Chi Holding a Ring Together
龙螭衔环谷纹青玉璧

15. Openwork-carved Dragon and Phoenix Bronze Door Knocker (from the site of Xiadu, the capital of the Yan State of the Warring States Period)

The bronze door knocker was unearthed in 1966 from the Laomu Terrace, the ruins of a large-scale palace complex, in the site of Xiadu, the capital of the Yan State in Yixian County, Baoding City. It stands 74.5 centimeters tall, measures 36.8 centimeters wide, and weighs 21.5 kilograms. It is now housed in Hebei Museum, being one of the top ten treasures of the museum and the largest bronze door knocker for palace gates in China.

Openwork-carved Dragon and
Phoenix Bronze Door Knocker
透雕龙凤纹铜铺首

Such door knockers (called "*Pushou*" in Chinese) were decorated on the gates of traditional Chinese architecture, with the purpose of warding off evil spirits. Ancient Chinese people believed that in order to prevent demons and monsters from entering their homes, one effective method was to place door knockers decorated with mythical creatures on their gates. In the past, decorative door knockers served as the most primitive form of door handles, allowing for opening and knocking on the door, while also serving a decorative purpose. Experts speculate that this bronze door knocker might have been a component of the palace gate in the site of Xiadu, the capital of the Yan State.

16. Blue and White, Underglaze Red Covered Jar with the Decoration Methods of Kaiguang[1] and Decal[2] (from the site of a cellar storage of the Yuan Dynasty)

The jar was unearthed in Baoding, Hebei. It stands 41 centimeters tall with the mouth diameter of 15.5 centimeters and the bottom diameter of

---

[1] Kaiguang is one of the composition methods of porcelain decoration. It is to outline circular, square, diamond, fan-shaped, cloud-shaped or floral shapes on the prominent parts of the utensils with lines, and paint various patterns in the frame, which serves to highlight the theme decoration.

[2] Ceramic decal is the most widely used decoration technique in ceramics. It is a method of transferring the colored pattern on the decal paper to the ceramic body or glaze surface by pasting.

Blue and White, Underglaze Red
Covered Jar with the Decoration
Methods of Kaiguang and Decal
青花釉里红开光贴花盖罐

18.5 centimeters. It is now housed in Hebei Museum.

The lid of the jar features a seated lion sculpture as the handle for opening the jar. The lid is adorned with blue and white lotus petal patterns, scroll patterns, and meander patterns, exhibiting exquisite craftsmanship and charm. From top to bottom, the wall of the jar becomes thicker, presenting a stout and robust appearance. The decorative elements are well-arranged, with the colors of blue, white and underglaze red complementing each other, creating a harmonious interplay of red and blue colors and rendering the jar elegant and graceful.

17. White-glazed Holy-water Vase with Incised Lotus Pattern and a Dragon-head Spout (from the Underground Palace under the foundation of the pagoda in Jingzhongyuan Temple of the Northern Song Dynasty)

This vase was unearthed from the Underground Palace under the foundation of the pagoda in Jingzhongyuan Temple of the Northern Song Dynasty in Dingzhou in 1969. It is now housed in Dingzhou Museum.

This vase is 60.9 centimeters high, with a belly diameter of 19.1 centimeters and a base diameter of 10.1 centimeters. It has a slender neck, with a rim in the middle of the neck. The upper part of the neck is decorated with the overlapping lotus petal pattern with petals facing upwards; the middle part of the neck is a round disc called *Xianglun* (*Xianglun*, a Buddhist term referring to the circular rings strung on the finial of a pagoda), which is decorated with the overlapping lotus petal pattern with petals facing downwards; the lower part of the neck is decorated with the bamboo-like pattern. The vase is round-shouldered and belly-bulging, and its bottom does not have a foot ring and is slightly concave inward. Its shoulder is decorated with the triple overlapping lotus petal pattern with petals facing downwards, and one side is sculpted with a dragon head on a short spout. The dragon holds up its head high, with angry eyes, an open mouth showing teeth, and a wisp of beard on its lower jaw. The upper belly of the vase is carved with entwined flowers, and the lower belly is carved with four layers of lotus petals facing upwards. The lines of the patterns are sharp and smooth, creating a bas-relief effect. Ding kiln products are mainly small objects, and large objects are very rare. However, this vase is tall and elegant in shape, with gorgeous decorations. It is the most exquisite product among Ding kiln porcelain.

18. He Hongjing's Tombstone with Inscriptions (Wandi Ancient Tombs)

The tombstone is 1.95 meters in length and 0.53 meters thick, making it by far the largest of the Tang Dynasty tombstones unearthed in China. The tombstone is simply designed and beautifully carved with vivid patterns and smooth lines. The inscription on the tombstone, which describes the life events of the dead, is engraved in regular script, with a total of 60 lines, 58 characters per line, totaling 3,800 characters. It is now housed in Damingfu Stone Carving Museum in Handan City.

White-glazed Holy-water Vase with Incised Lotus Pattern and a Dragon-head Spout
白釉刻花龙首净瓶

He Hongjing's Tombstone with Inscriptions
何弘敬墓志铭

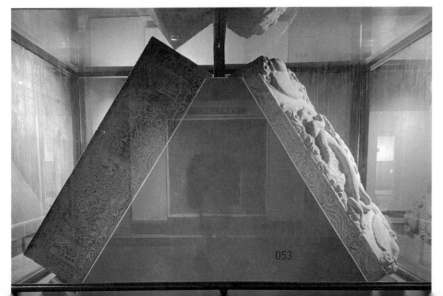

# Exercises

Ⅰ. Comprehension

（1）In which year were the Chengde Mountain Resort and the Eight Outer Temples selected as a World Cultural Heritage site?

（2）Why is it said that the most magnificent section of the Great Wall is in Hebei? Which section is it?

（3）How many sections does the Grand Canal pass through in Hebei? Which cities in Hebei does the Grand Canal pass through?

（4）How many imperial Qing tombs are there in total? How many are there in Hebei?

（5）Besides the 18 national treasures introduced in this division, what other cultural relics unearthed in Hebei do you know about?

Ⅱ. Translation

1. Term Translation

（1）铁画银钩

（2）南水北调

（3）古今枢纽

（4）皇家寺庙群

2. Passage Translation

作为京杭大运河流经最长的一座城市，沧州曾是商贾云集的南北通衢。人头攒动的码头，塑造了沧州的江湖气；"武术之乡"撑起中国功夫的半边天；火锅鸡、河间驴肉火烧则打下了河北美食的半壁江山。而随着大运河的没落，沧州的气质重新回归海洋。提及长芦盐场，首先想到沧州，同时，沧州也是我国最大的工业盐产地。沧州特产黄骅梭子蟹足以与舟山抗衡。沧州凭借黄骅港，被列为北方重要港口城市。再加上铁路、高速四通八达，让沧州成为名副其实的"冀鲁枢纽"。

Part Two
The Glorious Tradition of Revolution

Hebei has a glorious revolutionary tradition and history and is the hometown of Li Dazhao, one of the founders of the Communist Party of China. It is also one of the earliest provinces where the Communist Party of China organized. During the National Revolution (1924-1927), great and momentous struggles were undertaken in Hebei. During the War of Resistance against Japanese Aggression, Hebei became the main battlefield behind enemy lines, and Jin-Cha-Ji (Shanxi-Chahar-Hebei) War of Resistance Base Area, the first base behind enemy lines, was set up to the eastern side of Taihang Mountains in Hebei. The Jin-Cha-Ji Border Region Government and the 129th Division Command of the Eighth Route Army were located here. In order to crush the Japanese imperialist aggressors, the army and the people of Hebei creatively used tactics like tunnel warfare, landmine warfare, and guerrilla warfare on the plains to fight against the Japanese invaders, leaving behind important revolutionary relics such as the Ranzhuang Tunnel Warfare Site. During the Liberation War period, Hebei was not only the command center for the liberation of China, but also one of the main battlefields of the war. Xibaipo was the last rural command post in China, from where China embarked on a new journey. The revolutionary tradition is an indelible part of Hebei's glorious history and the revolutionary sites are the most distinctive cultural landscapes in Hebei.

Lead-in Questions

(1) During the War of Resistance against Japanese Aggression, the people of Hebei fought behind enemy lines relying on the Taihang Mountains. Do you know the history of that period?

(2) Before the establishment of the People's Republic of China, where was the last rural command post located?

(3) There are many revolutionary relics in Hebei. Have you visited any of them?

(4) The heroic martyrs of Hebei emerged in large numbers during the War of Resistance against Japanese Aggression and China's War of Liberation (1945—1949). Do you know any of them?

Chapter 7
Xibaipo

—The Starting Point of New China

The Hutuo River rushes all the way through Hebei, and when it reaches Pingshan County of Shijiazhuang in Hebei, it bends and embraces a tranquil village—Xibaipo.

Xibaipo, a small mountain village on the north bank of the Hutuo River in western Hebei Province, boasts beautiful scenery and fertile land. It was the location of the Central Working Committee (CWC) and the Central Committee of the Communist Party of China (CPC) as well as the headquarters of the People's Liberation Army (PLA) during the War of Liberation. It is

Bronze Statues of the Five Great Secretaries of Xibaipo, Pingshan County
平山县西柏坡 五大书记铜铸像

here that the CPC Central Committee and Chairman Mao Zedong directed the Liaoshen, Huaihai and Pingjin Campaigns, which determined the victory of the War of Liberation. Moreover, the Second Plenary Session of the Seventh CPC Central Committee as well as the National Land Conference was held in Xibaipo, which is of great historic importance. After that, the whole country was liberated and thus Xibaipo is known as "the Starting Point of New China" and "the village where China's destiny is determined".

In May 1947, the Central Working Committee led by Liu Shaoqi and Zhu De entered and garrisoned Xibaipo, and in May 1948, the CPC Central Committee and the headquarters of the PLA led by Mao Zedong, Zhou Enlai and Ren Bishi converged with the Central Working Committee, making Xibaipo the command center for the liberation of China at that time. Here, the National Land Conference of the CPC was held and *The Outline of the Land Law of China* was formulated, realizing the goal that the cultivator should own his field; the Three Major Campaigns, namely Liaoshen, Huaihai and Pingjin campaigns were strategically planned here, and the decisive victory of these strategic campaigns made this mountain village "the last rural command post for the liberation of the whole China"; the Second Plenary Session of the Seventh CPC Central Committee was held here, drawing up the grand blueprint for the new China. On March 23, 1949, the CPC Central Committee and the headquarters of the PLA left for Beijing for the establishment of New China.

After the departure of the CPC Central Committee, the government of Jianping County (later renamed Pingshan County in 1958) took over the items left behind by the CPC Central Committee. In order to protect the revolutionary sites and cultural relics, the Preparatory Office of Xibaipo Memorial Hall was established in 1955, and on March 11, 1982, the former site of the CPC Central Committee in Xibaipo was listed by the State Council as a national key cultural relic protection unit.

Since 1992, a series of educational projects for promoting revolutionary tradition have been built successively in Xibaipo, such as the Xibaipo Stone Carving Park, the Xibaipo National Security Education Hall, the Xibaipo Integrity Education Hall, the Leader's Sculptures Park, the Bronze Statues of the Five Great Secretaries, the Xibaipo Monument, the Monument of Zhou Enlai's Remarks, the Monument of Xibaipo Cultural Relics Protection, the Xibaipo Teenagers' Park for Ecological Conservation, which have greatly enriched patriotic education of the base. At present, the Xibaipo Patriotic Education Base has formed a complete and multi-level education system for promoting revolutionary tradition.

The former site of the CPC Central Committee in Xibaipo covers an area of 1,644 square meters and is enclosed by a gray-white earthen wall. Inside the compound are the former residence of Mao Zedong, Zhu De, Liu Shaoqi, Zhou Enlai, Ren Bishi and Dong Biwu, as well as 17 other sites including the command room of the Central Military Commission, the former site of the September Conference, and the former site of the Second Plenary Session of the Seventh CPC Central Committee. In these simple bungalows, the utensils once used by the leaders in their work and daily life are displayed. The faded desks, old-fashioned telephones, kerosene lamps, worn-out chairs and sofas, and stacks of military maps, etc. All of them represent the hard years of the older generation of revolutionaries in Xibaipo, and eulogize the brilliant achievements accomplished by those great people for the founding of New China.

The construction of the Xibaipo Exhibition Hall started in October 1976, and on May 26, 1978, to commemorate the 30th anniversary of the relocation of the CPC Central Committee and the headquarters of the PLA to Xibaipo, it was opened to the public along with the former site of the CPC Central Committee. The basic displays in the exhibition hall had been readjusted and renewed in 1993, 1996, 1998 and 2003, and had been rated in 1998 as one of the "National Top Ten Fine Displays" by the National Cultural Heritage Administration. The current basic display, titled "Xibaipo, the Starting Point of New China", won the "Special Award for National Top Ten Fine Displays" in 2003. The entire display consists of 12 exhibition rooms (including the lobby), starting with the events of the glorious struggle against Japanese aggression of the Pingshan people, taking the War of Liberation as the main theme, and demonstrating the revolutionary activities of the Central Working Committee and the CPC Central Committee in Xibaipo. It focuses on the major historical events such as the National Land Conference, the Three Major Campaigns, the Second Plenary Session of the Seventh Central Committee, etc. By utilizing high-tech exhibition methods such as sound, light, and electricity, as well as adopting modern exhibition concepts, the exhibition vividly highlights the theme of "Xibaipo, the Starting Point of New China".

Nowadays, Xibaipo has become a famous revolutionary tourism resort in China. The number of visitors has been increasing year by year. With a sense of reverence, visitors from all over the country come to Xibaipo to reminisce about the eventful years of the older generation of revolutionaries and seek the true essence of the Xibaipo spirit.

Chapter 8
The Ranzhuang Tunnels

—An Impregnable "Underground Great Wall"

The Ranzhuang Tunnel Warfare Site in Qingyuan District of Baoding City in Hebei, is an exemplary feat of the Chinese nation's triumph over a stronger enemy during the War of Resistance against Japanese Aggression. It is also a miraculous testament to the world's people's resistance against fascist aggression during the World War II. As time passes, the once smoke-

Ranzhuang Tunnel Warfare Site
冉庄地道战遗址村口

filled battlefield of the war against Japanese invaders has transformed into a beautiful place of peace and tranquility. However, "the Great Wall of Steel" buried underground is the testimony to those years, inspiring the future generations to move forward. In 1965, the revolutionary movie *Tunnel Warfare* was released, which not only became a classic, but also made Ranzhuang famous.

Walking within the protected area of the Ranzhuang Tunnel Warfare Site, the touching melody of the song *We Keep Chairman Mao's Words in Mind* echoes in visitors' ears, and everything appears calm and peaceful. However, the concealed firing ports on the ground, the various fortifications behind the high walls and residential buildings, and the winding underground "Great Wall", are all silently telling the story of those turbulent years.

The cross street in Ranzhuang Village has maintained the appearance of the 1930s and 1940s. The old Chinese scholar tree at the entrance of the village despite being withered, still stands tall. It is exactly the same tree in the movie *Tunnel Warfare* produced over 50 years ago, where the scene of Gao Laozhong, the village Party secretary, running quickly towards the Chinese scholar tree to ring the alarm bell was filmed. This old Chinese scholar tree has a history of over 1,000 years, and such ancient trees are rare in the Central Hebei Plain. It is said that at that time the old tree was flourishing, and it did indeed have an ancient clock hanging on it specifically used for alarm purposes. Nowadays, as a testimony to history and a precious cultural relic, the old tree has been reinforced with armoured concrete and has become a permanent site for revolutionary tradition education.

The tunnels in Ranzhuang, which embodies great wisdom, have several distinct features: the tall buildings are connected to each other and so are courtyards and tunnels; the concealed firing ports and exposed ones are deployed alternately, and so are bunkers and tall building fortifications as well as firing ports on the walls and firing ports of bunkers; it is easy to hide, move, fire and transfer to other places; the tunnels are also safe from blockade, sabotage, fire, flooding and poison gas. Inside the tunnels, there was a command post, some food storerooms and rest rooms, and several small-scale weapon factories and other facilities. The command post is located just underneath the cross street. Taking the cross street as center, the people of Ranzhuang dug four main tunnels along the east, west, south, and north streets and 24 branch tunnels, forming a tunnel network up to 32 *li* (1 *li*=0.5 kilometer), with concealed firing ports spreading throughout the village.

At that time, every village in the Central Hebei Plain had tunnels, and the total length was 25,000 *li*, making it a true "Underground Great Wall" and a miracle in the war history of China and even the world. These tunnels were really a miracle created by tenacious Chinese people on the vast plain, which has no natural defenses, under the brutal war condition.

The Ranzhuang Tunnel Warfare Site was listed as one of the first batch of national key cultural relic protection units by the State Council in 1961. It is also a national patriotic education demonstration base, a national education base for teenagers, one of the first batch of national defense education demonstration bases, and one of the top 100 classic revolutionary tourism scenic spots in China. In 2014, it was selected by the State Council as one of the first batch of national-level memorial facilities and sites of the War of Resistance against Japanese Aggression.

In September 2010, the new building of the Ranzhuang Tunnel Warfare Memorial Hall was officially opened to visitors. The total construction area of the new building is nearly 4,000 square meters, with an exhibition area of 1,800 square meters. The museum houses a large collection of precious revolutionary cultural relics, including 4 national first-level revolutionary cultural relics, 17 national second-level revolutionary cultural relics, and 77 nationel third-level revolutionary cultural relics. At the entrance of the exhibition hall, there is a wall of relief depicting the history from 1931 to 1945, which resembles a tunnel of time, bringing people back to those war-ridden years. The exhibition in the new building is themed "The Underground Great Wall, A Wonder during the War of Resistance against Japanese Aggression", showcasing the plight of the central Hebei region during the Japanese occupation, the sufferings of the Chinese people, the efforts of Chinese people to save the critical situation, and the mighty power of tunnel warfare that finally gained its international renown. The memorial hall combines modern design language with realistic landscapes, enriched with a large number of revolutionary cultural relics, photographs, charts, sculptures, and paintings. It utilizes various techniques and advanced technologies to make the exhibition more engaging and interactive.

The people of Ranzhuang, under the leadership of the CPC, fearlessly rose to fight in those hard times. According to the statistics, they utilized the advantage of the underground tunnels to fight against the enemies 157 times during the War of Resistance against Japanese Aggression and the War of Liberation, annihilating more than 2,100 enemies. Ranzhuang thus won the honorable title of "Model Village of Tunnel Warfare" and was designated as a national historical and cultural village in 2007. In 1950, delegations from 36 countries visited Ranzhuang and were amazed by the miraculous tunnel warfare. Now, Ranzhuang preserves a protected area of 300,000 square meters, and the number of visitors annually exceeds one million. The Ranzhuang Tunnel Warfare Site combines patriotic education, national defense education, and tourism, making it an ideal and unique destination and leaving behind a precious and eternal historical treasure for future generations.

Chapter 9
The Jin-Cha-Ji Border Region Revolutionary Memorial Hall

—Where the Embryonic Form of New China Was Shaped

The Jin-Cha-Ji Border Region Revolutionary Memorial Hall is located in Chengnanzhuang Town, Fuping County, Baoding City. It was formerly known as the Chengnanzhuang Revolutionary Memorial Hall, in which the former site of the Jin-Cha-Ji Military Region Command was listed as a provincial-level patriotic education base in 1994, a national-level key cultural relic protection unit in 1996, and a national patriotic education demonstration base in 2005.

Former Site of the Headquarters of the Jin-Cha-Ji Military Region
晋察冀军区司令部旧址

In 1937, Nie Rongzhen established the Jin-Cha-Ji War of Resistance Base Area with Fuping as the starting point, which was the first base behind enemy lines established by our Party and army. It was not only a strong "fortress" in the War of Resistance in North China, but also the front-line position for our army to launch strategic counter-offensives against Japanese invaders during the War of Resistance and for our army to march into Northeast China and seize North China during the War of Liberation. The innovative democratic system and the well-established organization structure created in the Jin-Cha-Ji Border Region accumulated invaluable experience for the establishment of New China. It was a model for the whole country in fighting against Japanese invaders during the War of Resistance, in implementing the Party's policies, in developing the united front, in constructing base areas, and in adopting the strategy of People's War (People's War is a war strategy that relies on the power of the masses, resisting the enemy through extensive mobilization and unconventional warfare methods. The concept of People's War was advocated by Mao Zedong and was widely applied during the Chinese War of Resisfance against Japanese Aggression and the War of Liberation). Therefore, Jin-Cha-Ji Border Region is called "the prototype of the new-democratic society" "the embryonic form of New China", and was awarded the honorary title of "the Model Base Area of the War of Resistance against Japanese Aggression" by Mao Zedong. In April 1948, Chairman Mao led the Party Central Committee to Chengnanzhuang, Fuping County in the Jin-Cha-Ji Border Region from northern Shaanxi. They lived and worked here for a long time, during which he held an expanded meeting of the Secretariat of the CPC Central Committee to review the situation and adjust the strategy of the southern war front, laying a solid foundation for the victory of the Three Major Campaigns. Chairman Mao also drafted *the Slogan to Celebrate the May 1st Labor Day in 1948*, which for the first time concretely depicted the blueprint of New China and became the mobilization order for the founding of New China.

The entire scenic area consists of the Exhibition Hall, the Sculpture Square, the former site of the Headquarters of the Jin-Cha-Ji Military Region, and an air-raid shelter in the back mountain, covering a total area of 147,000 square meters. The Exhibition Hall covers an area of 1,700 square meters, with a display line of 260 meters, exhibiting 259 cultural relics, 222 photos and 31 charts. The exhibition is divided into six parts, arranged according to the historical development from the establishment of the base area to the relocation of the CPC Central Committee to Jin-Cha-Ji. The theme of the first part is "Establishing the First Base Area of the War of Resistance against Japanese Aggression behind Enemy Lines", which focuses on the establishment of the first base area behind the enemy lines by the Eighth Route Army after it marched to North China and won the Pingxingguan Battle under the orders of the Party Central Committee during the War of Resistance against Japanese Aggression. The theme of the second part is "Persisting in Guerrilla Warfare behind the Enemy Lines", which focuses on the use of various forms of resistance by the Eighth Route Army and the people of the Border Region against the Japanese invaders, and tells the deeds of the martyrs and heroes during this war. The theme of the third part highlights the achievements of the Border Region in Party building, and in political, economic, educational and cultural construction. The theme of the fourth part is "Achieving Victory in the War of Resistance against Japanese Aggression", which focuses on the large-scale military exercises in the Jin-Cha-Ji Border Region and the series of battles conducted by the Jin-Cha-Ji Military Region troops from 1944 onwards in preparation for the counter-offensive against Japanese invaders. The theme of the fifth part, "Embarking on a New Journey in the War of Liberation", focuses on the victories of the Jin-Cha-Ji Field Army in the Battle of Qingfengdian and the Battle of Shijiazhuang, after the Kuomintang resorted to war rather than pursued peace. The theme of the sixth part is "The Relocation of the CPC Central Committee to Jin-Cha-Ji", which emphasizes Chairman Mao's arrival in the liberated areas of Jin-Cha-Ji in 1948, where the land reform was implemented, the expanded meeting of the Secretariat was held, and the Party, government, and military institutions in North China were established, laying the foundation for the victory of the Three Major Campaigns. The exhibition fully embodies the theme of "the Model Base Area of the War of Resistance against Japanese Aggression" and utilizes a large number of precious photos, cultural relics, as well as advanced audio, visual, and lighting techniques. It employs various forms such as landscape restoration, phantom imaging, touch screens, and sculptures to provide detailed and vivid explanations of the exhibition content, showcasing the heroic deeds and immortal contributions of the soldiers and civilians in the Jin-Cha-Ji Border Region to the liberation of the Chinese nation.

The Sculpture Square contains six sets of bronze sculptures: Nie Rongzhen and Mihoko, Red News Correspondents, Li Yong and the Demolition Team, Rong Guanxiu and the Wounded Soldiers, the International Friend Norman Bethune, and the Five Heroes of the Langya Mountain, which vividly reflect the glorious history of the Jin-Cha-Ji Base Area from different aspects.

There are two courtyards in the former site, which was built in the autumn of 1947 when Commander Nie Rongzhen led the headquarters of the Military Region to retreat from Zhangjiakou to Fuping. The site covers an area of 1,752 square meters. In the front courtyard stands a majestic bronze statue of Nie Rongzhen, Commander of the Jin-Cha-Ji Border Region, while the courtyard is planted with cypress, ginkgo, and banyan trees, with birds chirping among the branches, creating a serene and elegant atmosphere. The backyard is the former site of the headquarters of the Jin-Cha-Ji Border Region, including three rows of adobe houses. In 1948, the CPC Central Committee led by Mao Zedong and Zhou Enlai moved here from Yan'an. There are offices (also dormitories) for Mao Zedong, Zhou Enlai, Ren Bishi and other leaders of the Central Committee, as well as a warfare office, a telephone room and a conference room. This is the only well-preserved site of the former headquarters of Jin-Cha-Ji Border Region in Hebei and the only well-preserved former residence of Chairman Mao and other leaders before they left for Beijing. It still retains its original appearance and layout. To the northwest of the site, there is a 128-meter-long air-raid shelter, which was manually excavated by the soldiers of the engineering company of the Jin-Cha-Ji Border Region and is still well preserved.

The memorial hall enjoys a beautiful environment, with the Bodhisattva Ridge to the north and the Yanzhi River to the south. Back then, it is here that Chen Yi wrote the magnificent line "ten-year stationing by the Yanzhi River" for Nie Rongzhen. The surrounding area of the hall

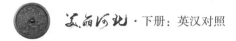

is adorned with lush pine and cypress trees, green grass, and blooming flowers. Outside the hall, there are towering green mountains and dense forests, creating a solemn and natural environment for visiting and relaxation.

Chapter 10
The "Little Grey House" in Shijiazhuang

—The Starting Point of New China's Financial Undertakings

At No. 55 Zhonghua North Street in the bustling city of Shijiazhuang, Hebei, there is a small three-story cement-brick building. It is cordially called the "Little Grey House" by locals because of its grayish appearance. This is where the People's Bank of China was established and where the first set of RMB was born.

The "Little Grey House" was first built in 1940 and initially served as the office building of the Japanese-sponsored General Administration of Construction in North China and the Shimen River and Canal Engineering Office (Shimen is the old name of Shijiazhuang.). After the surrender of Japan, the Kuomintang's advance troops occupied Shijiazhuang and used it as their headquarters. On November 12, 1947, after the liberation of Shijiazhuang, it became the office of the CPC Shijiazhuang Municipal Committee and was later handed over to the Bank of Ji'nan and the Bank of Jin-Cha-Ji Border Region. On December 1, 1948, the People's Bank of China officially set up its office here, and at the same time, the RMB was officially issued, making Shijiazhuang the first city to use the RMB as its currency.

In the process of the Communist Party of China (CPC) leading the Chinese nation to victory through hardships and difficulties, the financial work developed in tandem with the growth of the revolutionary power. From the Agrarian Revolutionary War to the War of Resistance against Japanese Aggression and until the eve of the founding of the People's Republic of China, the political power led by CPC was divided into separate and isolated base areas. Each area established its own relatively independent and decentralized bank, issuing currencies that circulated within each area. These early financial efforts played a unique and important role in the process of the Chinese revolution. This financial state did not change substantially until 1947, when the War of Liberation was about to change from strategic defense to strategic counter-offensive.

In order to overcome financial difficulties and guarantee war supplies, and to "mobilize all forces to prepare for the counterattacks", the North China Finance and Economics Conference was held in Yetao Town, Wu'an County, in the Jin-Ji-Lu-Yu (Shanxi-Hebei-Shandong-Henan) Liberated Area on March 25, 1947, with the approval of the CPC Central Committee. Representatives from the liberated areas attended the conference to discuss the issue of unifying finance and economics. To ensure ideological unity, Dong Biwu was sent by the Central Committee from northern Shaanxi to guide the conference. Dong Biwu, accompanied by his wife, children, and staff, traveled eastward. They ran out of provisions while passing through Wutai County, Shanxi Province. Dong Biwu took out the currency issued by the Shaanxi-Gansu-Ningxia Border Region Bank and asked a comrade accompanying him to buy food from a nearby store. However, the local people did not recognize the currency and refused to accept it. In the end, they had to use a piece of new cloth to exchange for food. Through this experience, Dong Biwu keenly felt the necessity and urgency of unifying the currency.

During the North China Finance and Economics Conference in April 1947, the CPC Central Committee decided to establish the North China Finance and Economics Office to unify the financial and economic policies of the liberated areas in North China and regulate their financial and economic relations. Dong Biwu was appointed as the director. On October 2, 1947, Dong Biwu telegraphed the CPC Central Committee, proposing the "establishment of a central bank and the issuance of a unified currency" and suggesting that the bank be named "the People's Bank of China". This proposal was positively affirmed by the CPC Central Committee. Subsequently, the Preparatory Office of the People's Bank of China was established in Jiayu Village, Pingshan County, with Nan Hanchen, who had previously served as the director of the Finance Department of the Shaanxi-Gansu-Ningxia Border Region and was currently the deputy director of the North China Finance and Economics Office, as the director of the Preparatory Office. With the liberation of Shijiazhuang, a major city in North China, and the approval of the higher authorities, the Ji'nan Bank and the Jin-Cha-Ji Border Region Bank were merged and relocated to the "Little Grey House" at No. 11 Zhonghua North Street (now No. 55 Zhonghua North Street) in Shijiazhuang on April 12, 1948. At the same time, the Preparatory Office of the People's Bank of China also moved from Jiayu Village, Pingshan County, to the "Little Grey House".

The comrades engaged in economic work were highly motivated and worked vigorously to establish the bank and print banknotes in preparation for the issuance of a unified currency. As early as before the November of 1947, the Banknote Printing Bureau of the Jin-Cha-Ji Border Region Bank had already completed several versions of the draft designs for banknotes. However, when the first set of RMB banknote designs with the portrait of Mao Zedong was submitted to the CPC Central Committee for review, Mao Zedong politely declined. He said, "The banknotes are to be issued by the government, not by the Party. Now I am the Chairman of the Party, not the Chairman of the government. Therefore, my portrait shouldn't be printed on the banknotes." So, Dong Biwu organized a redesign, proposing that the main pictures of the RMB should "reflect the industrial and agricultural production and construction scenes in the liberated areas". Finally, the first set of RMB banknote samples was designed by experienced designers Wang Yijiu and Shen Naiyong from the Banknote Printing Bureau of the Bank of Jin-Cha-Ji Border Region.

On December 1, 1948, the People's Government of North China announced the establishment of the People's Bank of China and the issuance of the new currency in the "No. 4 Monetary Notice". On the same day, the People's Bank of China was officially established in the "Little Grey House". After the first batch of RMB was printed, it was immediately sent to Xibaipo and presented to Mao Zedong by Dong Biwu for his review. Mao Zedong looked at the brand-new RMB and joyfully exclaimed, "The people now have their own armed forces, their own political power, their own land, and now they have their own bank and currency. This is truly the people being the masters of their own country!" On that day, the People's Bank of China officially issued the new currency with denominations of 10 yuan and 50 yuan both in Shijiazhuang and Pingshan County, marking the official birth of RMB. The first set of RMB consisted of 12 denominations and 62 designs, with the inscription "the People's Bank of China" written by Dong Biwu. This set of RMB ceased circulation in March 1955. The establishment of the People's Bank of China and the issuance of the first set of RMB are of epoch-making significance in the financial and monetary histories of China. It witnessed the process of the unification of the financial institutions and their currencies in the liberated areas on the eve of the victory of the New Democratic Revolution under the leadership of the CPC, putting an end to the decades of currency chaos under the Kuomintang's rule.

In January 1949, Beijing was peacefully liberated, and from February onwards, the People's Bank of China began to gradually move from the "Little Grey House" to Beijing. The Banknote Printing Factory, which was directly affiliated with the head office of the People's Bank of China, was relocated from Bailinzhuang in the northwest of Shijiazhuang to the "Little Grey House" to continue the printing of the first set of RMB. The Factory continued its work in the "Little Grey House" with the sign of "People's Bookstore" until the beginning of 1950, when the Factory merged with the Beijing People's Printing Factory and moved out of the "Little Grey House". Thus, the historical mission of the "Little Grey House" had come to an end for the time being.

After the completion of its restoration, the "Little Grey House" regained its splendid glory. On December 1, 2009, it was opened to the public with the brand new image of the Memorial Hall of the Former Site of the People's Bank of China and the Hebei Numismatic Museum, and was listed as a national key cultural heritage site and included in the list of "China's 20th Century Architectural Heritage Projects". The building bears witness to the beginning of China's financial industry in the new era and records that period of revolutionary history.

Chapter 11
The Pingshan Regiment

— "The People's Iron Army in the Taihang Mountains"

Pingshan County, Hebei Province, is located at the eastern foot of the Taihang Mountains and the upper reaches of the Hutuo River. It is a mountainous county in the western part of Shijiazhuang. The revolutionary holy site of Xibaipo is located in the middle of Pingshan County. When it comes to Xibaipo in Pingshan County, it is well-known to people for its reputation of "Xibaipo, the Starting Point of New China". This once-ordinary little mountain village has gone down in history as the pride of the people of Pingshan and even Hebei. Pingshan County also has a group that is worthy of pride and being recorded in history, and that is the Pingshan Regiment.

In the early 1930s, the revolutionary spark ignited in Pingshan County. At the end of 1934, Li Zaiwen, the first member to join the Communist Party of China in Pingshan County, returned to his hometown and participated in the leadership work of the CPC Pingshan County Committee. Since then, the revolutionary torrent surged and became unstoppable in Pingshan County. In September 1937, the Eighth Route Army, which had achieved a great victory at Pingxingguan on the front lines of the War of Resistance against Japan, marched eastward to open up resistance bases in the enemy's rear areas. Under such background, on September 28th, Wang Zhen, deputy commander of the 359th Brigade of the 120th Division of the Eighth Route Army, led his troops to Hongzidian Village in Pingshan County, where he conveyed to the CPC Pingshan County Committee the instructions from the Party Central Committee on establishing resistance bases and carrying out guerrilla warfare in the enemy's rear areas. He called on the Communist Party members in Pingshan County to organize the people of Pingshan to resist against Japan, and save the country and defend their hometown with their lives. Li Zaiwen, secretary of the CPC Jixi Special Committee (CPC Jixi Special Committee is a historical organization, which was established during the War of Resistance against Japanese Aggression, responsible for leading and guiding the work of resistance against Japanese invaders in the Jixi region. Jixi refers to the western part of Hebei Province.), and Wang Zhao, secretary of the CPC Pingshan County Committee, led the Communist Party members in Pingshan County to quickly form ten army-expansion teams, which were dispatched to villages and towns for publicity and mobilization. Pingshan County responded drastically. Slogans such as "Everyone has responsibility to resist the Japanese aggression and save our country" and "Join the Eighth

Pingshan Regiment Monument
平山团纪念碑

Route Army and drive away the Japanese invaders" resounded through the Taihang Mountains. Such slogans were seen everywhere, and the songs of resistance against Japanese invaders reverberated loudly all over the county.

What does it mean to join the Eighth Route Army? It means a willingness to sacrifice oneself for the country at any moment. Therefore, the Party members in Pingshan, who were rich in the spirit of sacrifice, took the lead in enlisting. Liang Yuqing, a member of the CPC Pingshan County Committee, mobilized the Party members in his hometown to enlist in the army. As a result, 34 people from Maoshi Village, a village that consisted only of 60 households, joined the Eighth Route Army. Liang Yuqing became the leader of the First Platoon of the First Company of the First Battalion of the Pingshan Regiment of the Eighth Route Army. Li Fazhuang, the first farmer Party member and the first rural Party branch secretary in Pingshan County, led more than 60 young people from Huobintai Village to join the army collectively in Hongzidian Village. Touching scenes of fathers and sons joining the army together, brothers joining the army together, and teachers and students joining the army together appeared in the mountain villages and towns of Pingshan. In just one month and three days, Pingshan recruits, ranging in age from 12 to over 50, joined the resistance forces against Japanese invaders one after another, forming a Pingshan Regiment of 1,700 soldiers. On November 7, 1937, amidst the exciting sound of gongs and drums, the Pingshan Regiment left Hongzidian Village and followed the 359th Brigade of the 120th Division to the front line of the War of Resistance against Japanese Aggression. In January 1938, Luo Ronghuan led the 115th Division Instructional Team to Hongzidian Village, hoping that Li Zaiwen would help expand the number of soldiers. The enthusiasm for joining the army surged again, and another 1,700 young people from Pingshan County joined the 115th Division and advanced into the southeastern part of Shandong Province, becoming the Pingshan Regiment of the 115th Division. According to statistics, during the War of Resistance against Japanese Aggression, Pingshan County, a county with a population of only 250,000, sent a total of 12,065 heroic soldiers to join the Eighth Route Army.

The Pingshan Regiment went to the front line, fought bravely, and had made great achievements in the war. On March 11, 1938, the 2nd Battalion of the 718th Regiment and the 717th Regiment besieged and destroyed the Chitanda Battalion (consisting of around 1,100 soldiers) of the Japanese 26th Division in Sanjing Town, Kelan County, killing and injuring more than 300 Japanese soldiers and capturing 28 Japanese soldiers; on June 10, the 2nd Battalion and the 3rd Battalion of the 718th Regiment engaged in a battle in Nanjinjiazhuang, Hunyuan County, trapping over 300 Japanese soldiers in a narrow strip of land. They concentrated their firepower and fiercely attacked them, killing and injuring more than 100 Japanese soldiers; from September 24th to 30th, Chen Zongyao, commander of the 718th Regiment, led the 1st Battalion and the 3rd Battalion to obstruct the Japanese troops attacking Lingqiu County. They occupied advantageous terrain, took advantage of the night-combat flexibility, pressed forward step by step, and even forced 100 Japanese soldiers to jump off the cliffs....

In November 1938, Zuo Qi, chief of staff of the 718th Regiment, was injured in the left arm during an ambush on a Japanese transport convoy. Dr. Norman Bethune performed emergency surgery on him overnight, dislocating his right shoulder joint to save his life. Dr. Norman Bethune also saw some other soldier from the 718th Regiment and when he learned that these young men were all from Pingshan, he was extremely surprised. He happily chatted with them and told the soldiers that he had just come from Pingshan. He pronounced the two characters " 平山 (Pingshan)" in stiff Chinese, which elicited laughter from the soldiers. Dr. Bethune had a deep affection for the Pingshan Regiment. In his diary and letters, he warmly referred to them as "simple and lovely children", and "working people in military uniforms". He recalled, "Their average age is twenty-two years old... They are usually big men, six feet tall, strong, dark-skinned, calm in every move, and with a clear purpose and a resolute demeanor. Serving them is indeed a kind of happiness..." Through Dr. Bethune's meticulous treatment, 71 wounded soldiers from the Pingshan Regiment returned to the front lines of the War of Resistance against Japanese Aggression.

In May 1939, the 717th Regiment was outflanked by the Japanese during their "mop-up" operation and the 718th Regiment rushed to their aid. In the battle, the 718th formed a counter-encirclement against the Japanese and engaged in a close-quarters combat. This battle lasted for seven days and nights, resulting in over 1,000 Japanese soldiers killed or injured. Among them, more than 600 enemy soldiers were killed, and 11 were captured. Wang Jiachuan, a soldier of the 3rd Battalion, alone killed 8 Japanese invaders. In addition, the regiment also captured 2 Type 92 infantry cannons, 3 mortars, 22 light and heavy machine guns, over 800 rifles, and more than 200 war horses. This battle brought out the prestige and fame of the Pingshan Regiment. The good news spread, and on May 20, Nie Rongzhen, commander of the Jin-Cha-Ji Military Region, issued commendation to the Pingshan Regiment, granting it the honorary title of "the people's iron army in the Taihang Mountains". He pointed out that "The officers and soldiers of the Pingshan Regiment have carried forward the glorious tradition of the Eighth Route Army. Despite all sacrifices, they resolutely annihilated the enemy deep in the mountains. This is the most glorious victory for all the soldiers of the Pingshan Regiment … You are the excellent representatives of Pingshan people, the excellent armed forces of the people of the Border Region, and the people's iron army in the Taihang Mountains!" This is the first time that the term "People's Army" was used to refer to the people's armed forces under the leadership of the Communist Party of China. On May 28, the full text of Nie Rongzhen's commendation order was published in the newspaper *Resistance Against the Enemy News*, and the terms "Pingshan Regiment" and "People's Army" quickly spread throughout North China.

Why did the term "People's Army" quickly become well-known? Because it was beloved by Chinese people and the officers and soldiers of the people's armed forces; because it contained the deep affection between the people's armed forces and the people, who were united together and shared weal and woe as an inseparable union; and because it profoundly exemplified the new type of military-civilian relationship that the people's armed forces under the leadership of the Communist Party of China originate from the people and are rooted in the people. Mr. Li Gongpu, a renowned democrat, visited the Jin-Cha-Ji region in the spring of 1940 and wrote the book *Behind the Enemy Lines in North China—Jin-Cha-Ji*, in which he praised that the people's armed forces were the troops rooted in the Jin-Cha-Ji region to resist Japanese invaders and they were the sons of the people. Since then, the term "People's Army" has spread throughout the country as an affectionate term for the people's armed forces under the leadership of the Communist Party of China, and has been used to this day.

Chapter 12

The Battle Along the Xifengkou Great Wall Against Japanese Aggressors

—The Broadswords Demonstrating the Unyielding Spirit of the Chinese Nation

Xifengkou, located in the north of Qianxi County, Tangshan City, is one of the many passes of the Great Wall of China. In 1933, a battle against foreign invasion broke out here where five hundred brave soldiers wielding broadswords swords struck the arrogant invaders, displaying the formidable spirit of the Chinese people! The Battle of Xifengkou has become a significant and memorable event in the history of China's War of Resistance against Japanese Aggression.

Xifengkou Great Wall Anti-Japanese War Monument
喜峰口长城抗战纪念碑

The site of the Battle along the Xifengkou Great Wall covers an area of 2800 *mu*. Centered around the historic event of the victorious Battle of Xifengkou in 1933, and featuring the cultural elements of patriotism such as the original location where the well-known patriotic song *The Broadsword March* was composed and the original location where the famous slogan "I'd rather die in battle than be a slave losing my country" was created, various historical and cultural landmarks have been constructed. These include the Xifengkou Great Wall Anti-Japanese War Monument, the Great Wall War of Resistance Poetry Memorial Wall, the sculpture themed "The Broadsword to Slash at the Enemy's Head", the Memorial with the inscription of "Remember History, Strengthen China", the War Martyrs Cemetery, the Xifengkou Great Wall War of Resistance Museum, the Xifengkou Great Wall War of Resistance Memorial Exhibition Hall, and the East Hebei War of Resistance Spirit Exhibition Hall.

After the September 18th Incident, the three provinces in Northeast China fell into Japanese's hands, and in March 1933, the Japanese invaders advanced towards the Great Wall, intending to break through at Xifengkou, which put Beijing and Tianjin in danger. Some patriotic generals such as Song Zheyuan and Zhao Dengyu quickly rushed to the vicinity of Xifengkou with the 29th Army of the National Revolutionary Army to resist the enemy, and desperately fought against the Japanese invaders.

In the glass display cases of the museum, the broadswords that once slaughtered the enemy still gleam with a chilling coldness, their blades are still sharp and shiny. Faced with the well-equipped Japanese invaders, the 29th Army selected 500 elite soldiers to form the Da Dao (Broadsword) Dare-to-Die Corps, determined to engage the enemy in close combat with their own lives, vowing to defend the homeland to the death. To boost morale, the army commander Song Zheyuan wrote the order "I'd rather die in battle than be a slave losing my country" and announced it to the whole army.

Late in the night on March 11, 1933, the commander Zhao Dengyu and the deputy commander He Jifeng of the 109th Brigade of the 29th Army led the members of the Da Dao Dare-to-Die Corps in a nocturnal assault on the enemy camp. At that time, the Japanese soldiers were deep in slumber. The members of the Da Dao Corps descended upon the enemy camp like divine soldiers, wielding their broadswords and beheading the enemies. The Da Dao Corps fought valiantly in the enemy camp for nearly three hours with the howls of 500 Japanese soldiers as their heads were sent flying.

According to historical records, the Battle of Xifengkou, with the night raid on the enemy camp as its representative, marked the first victory of the Chinese army against the Japanese invaders since the September 18th Incident. It was regarded as one of the classic examples in military history, demonstrating how a smaller and weaker force triumphed over a larger and stronger one. According to statistics, the Battle along the Xifengkou Grent Wall resulted in the cumulative destruction of over 5,300 Japanese soldiers, but the Chinese army also paid a tremendous sacrifice: 477 members of the Da Dao Dare-to-Die Corps laid down their lives for the country, with only 23 survivors.

The site of the Battle along the Xifengkou Great Wall has now been developed into the Xifeng Impregnable Pass Broadsword Park, becoming a classic revolutionary tourism scenic spot, a patriotism education base of Hebei, and a national defense education base of Hebei. The site has also been included in the second batch of national-level memorial facilities and site directories for the War of Resistance Against Japanese Aggression.

 Exercises

Ⅰ. Comprehension

（1）Where does the term "The People's Army" (人民子弟兵) come from?

（2）Which city was the first to use the Chinese currency RMB?

（3）Apart from the Battle along the Xifengkou Great Wall, do you know about the history of the War of Resistance in other parts of the Great Wall?

（4）Is there any other place in Hebei Province besides Ranzhuang in Baoding that has an underground tunnel warfare site?

Ⅱ. Translation

1. Term Translation

（1）滦州起义

（2）播火者

（3）烽火熔炉

（4）枕山襟海

2. Passage Translation

以巍巍太行为依托的晋冀鲁豫边区是华北敌后最大的抗日根据地。根据地的创建倾注着毛泽东、朱德、周恩来、刘少奇、彭德怀、刘伯承、邓小平、聂荣臻等老一辈革命家的心血，凝聚了八路军指战员和广大人民群众百折不挠、浴血奋战、不怕困难、团结御侮的民族精神和气节。因此，太行革命根据地是中国革命史上的一座丰碑，太行精神是中国共产党和中华民族的宝贵财富，是千百年来中华民族爱国精神的集中展现。

Part Three

The Century-long Journey to a New Era

Hard-working spirit is the fine character and spiritual trait of Hebei people. Carrying forward this spirit, the people of Hebei have created one extraordinary miracle after another in the cause of revolution, construction and reform.

From planting one or two trees to turning the entire region into a land covered by vast forests, the people of Saihanba have not only created a beautiful highland but also a "miracle of hard struggle". Today, the people of Saihanba continue to carry forward this spirit and are "writing a new legend" in the new era. This spirit of perseverance is increasingly becoming a tenacious working spirit of Hebei people.

With the planning and construction of Xiong'an New Area and the opening of the Beijing-Xiong'an Intercity Railway, this "City of the Future" is getting prosperous. The rapid and continuous development and progress of Xiong'an New Area reflects Hebei's courageous and forward-looking attitude.

Chongli, a small town to the north of the Great Wall in Hebei, has become a new venue for skiing. With the successful hosting of the 2022 Winter Olympics, ice and snow sports have begun to thrive here. The ice and snow industry is growing vigorously, and Hebei has made great achievements in both the organization of the Winter Olympics and the local development.

Li Baoguo, known as the "New Yugong1^① of the Taihang Mountains", devoted his life to turning the barren mountains green and improving the living standards of the people in mountainous areas. In Baoding University, there is a volunteers' team made up of young men and women who are dedicated to the education development of western China. These young men and women represent the passionate enthusiasm of contemporary young Chinese, who are willing to devote their lives to the development of our motherland. On the new journey towards achieving the second centenary goal of China, the people of Hebei are constantly making more brilliant achievements.

Lead-in Questions

(1) When did the history of the centenary endeavor of Hebei begin? What historical periods has it gone through?

(2) Do you know some great deeds done by Hebei people in the process of poverty alleviation in the eastern side of the Taihang Mountains in the new era?

(3) Please locate Saihanba on the map and research for more information about its forests, so as to understand the historical changes happening there.

(4) Try to find Jumo County of Xinjiang on the map and see how far it is from your city.

---

① "Yugong" literally means "a foolish old man", who comes from the Chinese fable "The Foolish Old Man Who Removed the Mountains". In the fable, Yugong was determined to remove two mountains blocking his village's path. Despite others doubting him, he persisted, believing that his dream would be realized some day. Impressed by his perseverance, the gods removed the mountains. The story of Yugong tells us that nothing is impossible if we work hard enough and if we are determined to accomplish our goals.

Chapter 13
The Centenary Endeavor
—Building a Prosperous Province

Hebei is a place with a glorious revolutionary tradition, a place where countless heroes have emerged, and a place where the People's Republic of China was once nurtured. It started to rise along the coast of the Bohai Sea, and has been developing together with the new China, constantly making amazing achievements one after another.

In 1952, the GDP of Hebei Province was only 4.05 billion yuan. In 1978, it reached 18.31 billion yuan. In 1991, 2005, and 2010, it achieved historical breakthroughs of 100 billion yuan, 1 trillion yuan, and 2 trillion yuan, respectively. In 2021, it exceeded 4 trillion yuan.

Dragon Train—Collection of Kailuan Museum
龙号机车——开滦博物馆馆藏

The industrial structure adjustment in Hebei has achieved a historic transformation, with the tertiary industry surpassing the primary and secondary industries to become the largest contributor to the regional GDP in 2018. During the "13th Five-Year Plan" period, the added value of high-tech industries grew at an average annual rate of 11.2%, and the proportion of the digital economy in Hebei's GDP exceeded 30%.

The coordinated development of the Beijing-Tianjin-Hebei region, the planning and construction of the Xiong'an New Area, and the successful hosting of the Beijing Winter Olympics have brought valuable historical opportunities and tremendous momentum for the development of Hebei. These major national strategies and events have had a significant impact on Hebei.

The process of Hebei's century-long efforts in development towards prosperity is a historical microcosm of the Chinese nation's transformation from weakness and pain to rise and glory.

More than a hundred years ago, the Chinese nation was in a difficult situation, and the people were struggling in suffering.

"To achieve the goal of constructing and restoring national autonomy, protecting the interests of the people, and developing the national industry...", revolutionary pioneer Li Dazhao, a native of Laoting of Hebei, made his final cry in his work *Self-Narration in Prison* in 1927.

In 1949, with the solemn proclamation of Chairman Mao Zedong on the Tian'anmen Gatetower, the People's Republic of China was born, and the Chinese nation embarked on a new historical era.

However, at the starting point of creating this miracle of development, China was faced with a scene of "desolation everywhere and everything waiting to be revived". Chairman Mao Zedong once said with deep emotion, "What can we make now?... We can't make a car, an airplane, a tank, or a tractor."

Poverty is not socialism! Without steel, there would be no high-rise buildings, vehicles, ships, guns, and cannons, let alone the modernization of China and the prosperity of the Chinese people's life. In 1957, the state decided to expand and build 3 large, 5 medium, and 18 small steel enterprises, with Handan Steel Plant being the only listed project in Hebei. Since then, several steel plants have been planned and built throughout the province.

Relying on the abundant iron ore resources of the Yanshan Mountains and the Taihang Mountains, the steel industry in Hebei has risen rapidly. In 1972, Hebei began to become an industrial powerhouse, with the secondary industry steadily surpassing the primary industry. Entering the new century, Hebei has become the largest steel-producing province in China, with production breaking through the 100 million ton mark, successively surpassing Germany, the United States, and Japan.

However, in the midst of this glorious process, risks have also accelerated their paces. In 2008, due to the impact of the international financial crisis and overcapacity, the profit margin of the steel industry plummeted. At the same time, energy consumption and environmental pollution were becoming increasingly severe, so the transformation of the steel-producing Hebei was imminent.

In that year, Tangshan Steel Group and Handan Steel Group merged to form Hebei Steel Group, and the concentration of the province's steel industry was greatly enhanced.

In 2013, the country began to resolve the problem of overcapacity in the steel industry. Hebei, with effective measures, the courage to make painful decisions, and the determination to fight for survival, launched a tough "battle" to deal with the problem of production overcapacity.

Resolutely reducing production capacity and then developing new space, mainly focusing on the six major industries of steel, coal, cement, flat glass, coke, and thermal power, Hebei had exceeded the capacity reduction targets set for the "13th Five-Year Plan" period. The steel production capacity had been reduced from the peak of 320 million tons to within 200 million tons, basically achieving the goal of relocating steel plants to places outside the cities. A total of 150,700 workers had been resettled, with a 100% resettlement rate.

Proactively adjusting and shifting to new industrial development directions, Hebei has put forward many new ideas in the field of industrial design, and tens of thousands enterprises have achieved remarkable results in their transformation. It has focused on cultivating 12 provincial-level leading industries and 107 county-level characteristic industries. The Great Wall cars produced in Baoding have become a benchmark for the national

The South Lake Park of Tangshan

唐山 南湖公园

automobile industry. The high-speed trains produced in Tangshan won the gold medal of the China Outstanding Industrial Design Award.

In order to accelerate transformation and promote high-quality economic development, in October 2019, the first China International Digital Economy Expo was held in Zhengding, Shijiazhuang. During the "13th Five-Year Plan" period, the contribution rate of scientific and technological progress in the province increased from 46% to 60%, and the number of high-tech enterprises reached 9,400. In 2020, the average concentration of PM2.5 in the province decreased by 56.9% compared to 2013, and the people can enjoy more nice weather now.

Having endured the pain of transformation, Hebei has eventually embraced the joy of sublimation.

During the "13th Five-Year Plan" period, the structure of the three industries in Hebei was optimized to 10.7:37.6:51.7, the per capita disposable income of residents increased from RMB 18,118 to RMB 27,136, the production of dairy products ranked first in China, the energy consumption per unit of GDP dropped by 21.26%, and the main economic indicators were higher than those of the national average. Historic new progress and changes had been made in various undertakings.

Under the impact of the COVID-19 pandemic along with the profound changes unseen in a century, Hebei has demonstrated a strong development resilience. The structural adjustment between industries has achieved historic breakthroughs, and the internal structural adjustments of industries have also developed steadily and rapidly.

The primary industry has been transformed from the traditional agriculture dominated by single crop farming to modern agriculture that involves multiple industries. The secondary industry has become more important, with the value-added growth of strategic new industries in 2020 increasing by 7.8%, which was 3.1 percentage points higher than that of "the above-scale industrial enterprises" ("The above-scale industrial enterprises" refer to industrial enterprises with an annual output value of over 20 million yuan.). The modern service industry has grown rapidly, with a contributing rate of 75.2% to the growth of the tertiary industry in 2018.

Today's Hebei is being guided by the new concept of innovative, coordinated, green, open and shared development, promoting the magnificent transformation from a province with huge potential to a province with powerful economy.

⛷ Chapter 14
Chongli

—A Town That Flourishes Due to the Winter Olympics

On July 31st, 2015, Beijing won the bid to host the 24th Winter Olympic Games in 2022. Beijing, once known for its successful bid for the 2008 Summer Olympic Games, rose to the global spotlight once again, this time with Chongli, a town in Zhangjiakou.

Unlike the Summer Olympics, the Winter Olympics have stringent weather requirements. Wind speed and strength, temperature, and visibility all directly affect the performance of athletes. In order to meet these requirements, the International Olympic Committee has made extremely strict criteria in selecting host cities. The core meteorological indicators for the Winter Olympics are twofold: the average temperature in February must be below 0°C, and the snowfall in February must be greater than 30 centimeters. Any city with a probability of less than 75% for either of the two indicators is not entitled to apply. Reviewing the previous Winter Olympics, you will see that almost all the host cities are basically located between 40°N and 70°N. Chongli of Zhangjiakou, located at 41°N, which is on the "World's Golden Ski Belt", has unique natural conditions that can fully meet the criteria of hosting the Winter Olympic Games.

The successful hosting of the 2022 Beijing Winter Olympics on February 4 brought Chongli into the spotlight of the world.

Chongli, the Zhangjiakou Area of the Beijing Winter Olympic Games, undertook two major events and six sub-events, and was the area that would produce the most gold medals. As the Winter Olympics progressed, more and more athletes came to Chongli, and more and more attention was drawn to this small town. From the preparation of the Olympic Games before 2022 to today, the changes in Chongli have gone beyond our imagination, vividly demonstrating Chinese efficiency, Chinese vitality, and the incredible development speed of China.

The literal meaning of "Chongli" is "advocating etiquette". As one of the districts of Zhangjiakou City, it used to be one of China's poverty-stricken areas. By the end of 2015, the official statistics still showed a local poverty rate as high as 16.81%.

Chongli is located in the transitional zone between the Inner Mongolian Plateau and

National Ski Jumping Center
张家口崇礼区 国家跳台滑雪中心 "雪如意"

the North China Plain, at the intersection of the Damaqun Mountain's residual ridges, which is the eastern part of the Yinshan Mountains, and the Yanshan Mountains' residual ridges. Here, there are rolling mountains and dense forests, and cold air from the northwest and warm, humid air streams from the southeast are lifted by the terrain, causing precipitation. At the same time, the high forest coverage, sufficient water vapor in the air, and excellent vegetation in Chongli are all conducive to the formation and storage of snow. 80% of Chongli's terrain is mountainous, with undulating terrain and moderate slopes, and its lowest temperature can reach minus 40 degrees Celsius. Early snowfall, deep snow accumulation, and a snow storage period of up to 150 days were once considered unfavorable conditions that prevented local people from getting out of poverty and becoming rich. However, in the eyes of experts, they have become advantages for Chongli's development.

　　With the Winter Olympics successfully hosted in this mountainous area, Chongli's development has entered the fast lane. The Winter Olympics have changed Chongli's fate, transforming it from a unknown small town into an prosperous place. Through the preparations for the Winter Olympics, Chongli's infrastructure has improved, and its ecological environment has become more beautiful.

In 2019, Chongli withdrew from the list of poverty-stricken counties, lifting itself from poverty completely. On December 30 of that year, the Beijing-Zhangjiakou High-speed Railway, the world's first intelligent high-speed railway with a speed of 350 kilometers per hour, was opened to traffic, marking the Zhangjiakou's entry into the Beijing-Tianjin-Hebei "one-hour living circle". The trip between Beijing and Chongli was shortened from over three hours to 50 minutes, bringing the two places closer in space.

The transformation of the small town of Chongli is not only a highlight of China's rapid development of ice and snow sports, but also a true reflection of the impact of the Winter Olympics on driving regional development and promoting all-round progress, including the well-being of the local people.

Currently, Chongli has as many as seven large ski resorts with 169 ski runs, including 15 advanced ski runs that have obtained international certifications. With the arrival of skiing enthusiasts and the rapid development of the skiing industry, various tourism facilities such as hotels, restaurants, and ski equipment shops have sprung up like mushrooms, and the city's infrastructure and image have also become increasingly better.

Chongli made the Olympics more successful, and the Olympics have made Chongli more beautiful. Undoubtedly, the Winter Olympics have brought about earth-shaking changes to Chongli. So, what has happened to Chongli since the Winter Olympics? With convenient transportation, improved supporting facilities, and upgraded ski resorts, Chongli after the Winter Olympics has attracted more people to come and experience what it feels like to ski in "the most ideal natural ski resort in North China".

In fact, the people of Chongli are also constantly thinking and taking action. Currently, one out of every three people in Chongli is engaged in sports and skiing-related work, and more than 40,000 people have directly or indirectly entered the ice and snow industry and tourism industry, being involved in snow-related activities. In the future, Chongli will closely focus on the sustainable utilization of Olympic facilities left behind after the Olympic Games, continue to accelerate the construction of the Beijing-Zhangjiakou Sports and Cultural Tourism Belt, vigorously develop sports and leisure industries led by winter skiing and summer outdoor activities, and work hard to promote the popularity and reputation of the city brand of "Chongli, a Snow World, and an Outdoor Paradise".

As spring returns to the earth and everything comes to life, the small town of Chongli is getting more and more beautiful.... In the past, this place would be trapped in ice and snow during winter; now, the ice and snow have brought it endless development opportunities.

This is Chongli, a charming town to the north of the Great Wall.

Chapter 15

The Western Education Supporting Team of Baoding University

—A Group of Young People Dedicating Their Youth to Western China

On April 25, 2014, General Secretary Xi Jinping wrote back to the representatives of the graduates of the Western Education Supporting Team of Baoding University, applauding their perseverance, dedication, hard work, and contribution. He encouraged young people to follow their examples, go to the grassroots and work for the people, let the flowers of youth bloom where the motherland needs them most, and make different but wonderful life choices in the great journey of realizing the Chinese Dream.

Reply Stone
保定学院校园内回信石

The Western Education Supporting Team of Baoding University is an outstanding representative of contemporary youth. After being reported in early 2014, their deeds have gained widespread attention. This group has received honorary titles such as "China's Good People Group for Dedication and Devotion" by the Central Civilization Office, "The Education Supporting Team that Pays Special Attention to Rural Areas" by *Guangming Daily* and CCTV, "March 8th Red Flag Group" of Hebei Province, and "China Youth May Fourth Medal Group" by The Central Committee of the Communist Youth League of China.

After spreading out the map, inch by inch, Hou Chaorou finally found a small black dot in the southeast corner of the Taklamakan Desert: Jumo, a small county so far away from Baoding, but a vast world in her eyes.

On March 30, 2000, Jumo No. 2 Middle School began recruiting teachers at Baoding University. At this time, the Western Development Campaign had just begun. Duan Jun, the principal of Jumo No. 2 Middle School at the time, introduced at the recruitment lecture that six of the seven classes in Grade One of the school do not yet have a head teacher. He called out loudly, "The children there need you!" Many students were immediately struck by the idea that youth is the most valuable when it is needed. Hou Chaoru immediately signed the contract and wrote in her diary, "Go to the West! I would like to spend my youth on the wilderness of life, regardless of the storms and lightning." Her parents were reluctant to let her go and gave her silent treatment for a month. It wasn't until the moment before departure that her mother finally hugged her, crying out loud.

On August 5, 2000, 15 spirited graduates with the banner that read "Go to the west to teach" boarded the westbound train amidst the cheers and farewells from the students and teachers of their alma mater.

"They left with their household registration." Hu Lianli, secretary of the Party Committee of Baoding University, recalled, "At that time, the Voluntary Service Program for University Students to work in the Western Region had not yet been launched, and there were no special preferential policies for going to work in the west." As pioneers of the Western Education Supporting Team, their stories became a hot topic of conversation spreading on the campus.

Xun Yina's English class began, her voice hoarse and low. The students listened attentively, as usual, with the hot water and throat lozenges prepared on the podium, along with a small note that read, "Ms. Xun, it's windy and sandy again. Please drink more water and speak in a low voice."

Just three months after arriving at the school, one day, Xun Yina suddenly couldn't speak in class. She was diagnosed with damage to her vocal cord due to the dry weather and excessive use of throat.

With 18 classes a week and teaching nearly a hundred students of three classes, Xun Yina was always occupied. And the sandy weather in Jumo County was the greatest challenge she and her colleagues faced.

Jumo is the second largest county in China in terms of area, with nearly 40% of its land covered by desert. The annual precipitation is less than 20 millimeters, and there are nearly 200 days of sand and dust weather each year. During sandstorms, the whole world becomes chaotic, and people can't see each other clearly even just one meter apart.

When you eat noodles, sand fills your mouth first; when your house is filled with floating dust, you have to cover your mouth and nose with a wet towel; cracked lips, swollen throats and nosebleeds are common occurrences for people working here....

They finally understood the words of Principal Duan Jun: the school had recruited teachers from various places, but after a sandstorm, a few would always be "blown away". However, they didn't leave. On the contrary, they felt more and more compassionate towards the children here. "Our minds are completely occupied by student's affairs. After class, we often share our teaching experiences and then bury ourselves again in preparing new lessons and correcting students' homework," Li Guizhi, one of the teachers of the supporting team, recalled. In the first semester, to improve her teaching skills, she attended more than 50 classes despite her heavy teaching load and wrote down a lot of notes.

While delivering history lessons in a clear and concise manner, Hou Chaoru also self-studied and obtained a national second-level qualification as a psychological counselor. She provides psychology classes and counseling for children who need psychological care. The students love her office where their secrets could be told, and whenever they have trouble, they would go to Teacher Hou and seek help from her.

Xun Yina locked up the doctor's medical advice in her drawer. She continued to teach as usual. The recurring symptoms of "vocal cord nodules" and "vocal cord incomplete closure" would sometimes require her to wear a microphone and headphones, and sometimes, she would have to teach by only writing on the board....

In 2003, the first batch of junior high school students they taught graduated. For the first time, the students' scores in the high school entrance examination ranked among the top in the entire Bazhou region, changing the situation that the education of Jumo County had always been the worst in this region!

Hou Chaoru's greatest happiness is seeing her student, Zhou Wenfei, becoming one of her colleagues now.

In 2013, Zhou Wenfei graduated from Xinjiang Normal University. She returned to Jumo and became a teacher. "I want to stand with Ms. Hou," she said. Setting up scholarships with their own money, taking care of sick students attentively.... The love and care given by these warm-hearted teachers are everywhere in Jumo County.

Of course, there is also a lot of warmth and love from the local people surrounding these volunteers.

The area in front of the school gate was cleaned up, and the teachers and students stood neatly in line to show their respect and welcome to these volunteers coming from afar. During a sudden earthquake, there was a pair of small hands of a student reaching out towards the teacher who stayed behind the students and organized the evacuation, saying, "Run together with us!" There were bags of potatoes carried by students over 40 kilometers, specially made baked buns by parents, and the biggest and sweetest pears from their homes.... Those who love others will receive love in return. This piece of western land, moistened by their sweat, has also given them wonderful rewards. They have achieved fruitful results in their careers. Most of them have grown up to become leading teachers and school administrators, and the teaching methods they created have been widely promoted in the schools throughout Bazhou, Nanmulin, and other places.

Their parents are becoming more and more understanding and

supportive. Some parents have moved here to live with their children, becoming "border area families". Some parents once wrote a long letter to their children, saying, "We understand your choice. Do not have the feeling of 'lack of filial piety'.... Teaching and cultivating talents for the border area is the greatest form of filial piety!"

"We have chosen to be ordinary, but not mediocre.... We are willing to be like red willows, like Galsang flowers, deeply rooted in the western region, resilient, willing to endure hardships, living a down-to-earth life, bringing boundless vitality to this vast land!" They wrote in a letter to General Secretary Xi Jinping.

As of 2021, 26 graduates from Baoding University have made the selfless decision to reside and work in the western region, offering their compassion and devotion to those in the border areas, while also pursuing their aspirations and ambitions within the vast expanse of the west.

Chapter 16
The Yuefeng Canal
—A Miracle in the Taihang Mountains

In the early years of the founding of the People's Republic of China, the western and southern parts of Cixian County, located on the northern bank of the Zhanghe River, suffered from barren land and frequent droughts. Water resources were scarce, and only one season of crops could be planted every year, with a yield of less than 200 jin (1 jin=0.5 kilograms) per mu (1 mu=0.164,7 acres). Faced with this situation, with the strong support of the Handan Special Administration Office, the County Committee of Cixian County decided to break through the Taihang Mountains and introduce water from the Zhanghe River with the ambition of "rearranging the rivers and mountains" to change the impoverished and backward conditions of the area. This decision made the Yuefeng Canal the first large-scale water diversion project to be built in the upper reaches of the Zhanghe River.

However, due to the outbreak of the Three Years of Natural Disasters in China, the construction of the Yuefeng Canal had to be temporarily suspended in 1960. In the same year, the Hongqi Canal in Linxian County, Henan Province, which also diverts water from the Zhanghe River, announced its commencement. Six years later, in 1966, the construction of the Yuefeng Canal resumed. Since then, it had undergone several times of large-scale reconstruction, expansion, and lining. The project was not completed until 1977. The main canal crosses mountains and leaps over ridges, bypasses obstacles and crosses ravines, diverting water from the Zhanghe River to the Fuyang River. Along the way, 28 mountains were cut through, and 74 gullies were crossed. A total of 178 large structures, including crossings, tunnels, culverts, and bridge gates, were built. It is known as the "Man-made River in the Sky".

The Yuefeng Canal starts from the Xiaosanxia Gorge of the Zhanghe River in the west and extends to the Dongwushi Reservoir in the east. The main canal has a total length of 57.2 kilometers and a designed irrigation area of 350,000 mu (about 23,333 hectares). The average annual water diversion is 100 million cubic meters, and a total of 6.3 billion cubic meters of water has been diverted so far. It benefits 10 townships, 197 villages, and a population of

295,000 in Cixian County. Over the past half century, it has developed into a large-scale water conservancy project with agricultural irrigation as its main function, integrating functions such as providing drinking water for humans and livestock, flood control, power generation, and industrial water supply. It has played an important supporting role in the agricultural and industrial production and economic development of Cixian County, and has provided important guarantees for industrial water supply and ecological replenishment in Handan City.

After entering the new century, as the drought situation worsens year by year, the Yuefeng Canal took on new tasks. Especially in 2009 and 2010, Cixian County experienced severe drought, with significantly reduced precipitation. The water level of Dongwushi Reservoir continuously declined, posing difficulties for fish farming in the reservoir area and industrial water demand in Handan City. Emergency water

Yuefeng Canal Monument
邯郸 跃峰渠纪念碑

diversion was urgently needed for Dongwushi Reservoir. Both the governments of Handan City and Cixian County issued instructions for emergency water transfer to Dongwushi Reservoir. At this critical moment, the local government officials took decisive measures, actively formulated water delivery plans, and twice transferred a total of 29.2801 million cubic meters of water from the Zhanghe River to Dongwushi Reservoir, making important contributions to the water supply needs of Handan City.

On July 19, 2016, Cixian County encountered a once-in-a-century heavy rainstorm, causing collapse and sedimentation in various sections of the Yuefeng Canal, damaging some structures, and rendering the canal paralyzed. There were 21 major places damaged and a total of 108 places affected. The canal lost its functions of water diversion, water delivery, irrigation, and water supply. The once beautiful "Man-made River in the Sky" was in ruins....

Faced with the unprecedented rainstorm disaster, all the officials and workers of the Yuefeng Canal in Cixian County carried forward the spirit of "self-reliance and arduous struggle" without any hesitation. Under the strong leadership of the CPC County Committee and County Government, they immediately organized all staff to clean up the channels such as the Yangcheng section, the Xinzhuang tunnel, the Liqing section, the Qingheyu section and the Fumagou section, clearing a total of nearly 100,000 square meters of silt, dredging nearly 20 kilometers of channels, temporarily repairing 10 regulating gates and spillway gates along the main canal and restoring the opening and closing functions of the canal.

Today, the Yuefeng Canal in Cixian County has already restored to its past appearance. The water-carrying capacity of some canal sections even exceeds the level before the disastrous event of the July 19, 2016. The indomitable spirit of the Yuefeng Canal has been injected with a new connotation in the new era. All the officials and workers of the Yuefeng Canal, together with the 500,000 people of Cixian County, are working harder in water conservancy construction in the new era!

Chapter 17
The Poverty Alleviation Efforts of Li Baoguo
—The "New Yugong of the Taihang Mountains"

For 35 years, Li Baoguo had been busy working in the Taihang Mountains, striving to find a way out of poverty for the local people. He worked hard to use science and technology to change the barren mountains and ridges into a place with a green and ecologically friendly environment. Every year, he spent more than 200 days working in the mountains like a farmer, only taking buns and boiled water as his meals. With a strong sense of responsibility, he determined to change this poor mountainous area into a prosperous and civilized place. Li Baoguo, the "People's Role Model" and the "new Yugong of the Taihang Mountains" in the new era, had pioneered a new path for poverty alleviation in mountainous areas.

Born in 1958 in a rural family in Wuyi County, Hengshui City, Hebei Province, Li Baoguo graduated from Hebei Forestry College (the predecessor of the College of Forestry, Hebei Agricultural University) in 1981. As one of the first batch of college students after the resumption of the college entrance examination, Li Baoguo became a teacher in his college after graduation. After only about 10 days at work, he plunged into the Taihang Mountains with his colleagues and began to conduct research on mountainous area development.

The Taihang Mountains have stones everywhere, and here the most scarce resource is land. In the Qiannanyu Village in Xingtai City, Hebei Province, Li Baoguo stared into these rocky mountains and determined to challenge them. He ran through all the ravines and gullies of the mountains and believed that blasting land leveling (Blasting land leveling is a method of land development and reclamation that uses blasting techniques to break up soil, rocks, and other surface materials, thereby achieving the purpose of leveling the land and improving land conditions. This method is commonly used in areas with complex terrain and hard soil texture, making it easier for construction, infrastructure development, or agricultural cultivation.) was a promising method of land improvement. When the soil layer became thicker, the soil and water were retained, and the survival rate of trees increased from the original 10% to 90%. On this basis, Li Baoguo began to guide farmers to plant chestnuts. In just a few years, Qiannanyu

Village not only became a well-known wealthy village but also one of the "greenest places in the Taihang Mountains".

Starting from changing Qiannanyu Village, Li Baoguo had settled his "home" in the Taihang Mountains. To help the people of Gangdi Village in Xingtai City out of poverty, Li Baoguo devoted himself to the research of apple planting and developed a 128-step standardized production and management process for apple cultivation. With apple farming alone, the villagers' per capita annual income had increased from less than 100 yuan to more than 30,000 yuan around 2015.

Yang Shuangniu, secretary of the Party Branch of Gangdi Village, recalled, "He really cared about the poor living conditions of the farmers here and worked with all his heart. He often got up early and stayed up late, climbing up the mountains and doing his research no matter how bad the weather was. He was strict with himself and asked his students to do the same. We appreciate his efforts very much and are very thankful for what he had done for us. As a university professor, he worked so hard to help our farmers. Our thankfulness is beyond words."

"As a member of the Communist Party of China, I must serve the people; as a teacher, I must serve the students." This is Li Baoguo's mantra, and also a true portrayal of his teaching work. In order to enable students to better combine theory with practice, Li Baoguo often "drove" a large number of students to the fields. He said, "To do scientific research, you have to be like farmers planting crops. You need to work hard and be down-to-earth. If you can't get yourselves rooted into the soil, you can't become real talents that are needed by our country."

How to link scientific research closely with practice? Li Baoguo's wife, Guo Suping, a researcher at the College of Forestry of Hebei Agricultural University, answered this question. She said, "The economic forestry specialty should be close integrated with practice. Baoguo's efforts in those mountainous agricultural experimental fields had brought great benefits to farmers, helping them find a way out of poverty and become rich. At the same time, he constantly updated the teaching materials and teaching content, making students interested in his classes."

Li Baoguo had been engaged in scientific research for a long time, and had made a lot of scientific research achievements and gained rich practical experience. He understood the forefront of the discipline, the needs of rural areas and the expectations of fruit farmers. He timely enriched his teaching content with his scientific research achievements and the experience he gained in practice, and timely updated the latest information in the field of production in his teaching.

On April 10, 2016, Li Baoguo passed away due to a sudden heart attack, leaving behind his family, students, and the farmers he cared much in the Taihang Mountains forever. Over the past 30 years, Li Baoguo had completed 28 research achievements in mountainous area development, and 18.26 million mu of land had benefited from the promotion and application of his technology. He turned 1.4 million mu of barren mountains into a green forest, and helped to increase the income of mountain farmers by 5.85 billion yuan. However, he didn't seek for personal interests, neither accepting the remuneration from the farmers nor the shares of the enterprises. Throughout his life, he maintained the integrity and selfless dedication spirit of a communist.

Li Baoguo was posthumously awarded the titles of "National Excellent Communist Party Member" "Reform Pioneer" "The Most Outstanding Contributor" "Model of the Times", and "National Model for Poverty Alleviation". In 2019, he was also granted the honorary title of "People's Role Model" by the state.

Chapter 18
Saihanba Mechanized Forest Farm
—A Model of Chinese Ecological Civilization Construction

In the northern part of Chengde City, Hebei Province and the southern edge of the Hunshandake Sandy Land in Inner Mongolia lies a 1.15 million mu man-made forest, known as the Saihanba Mechanized Forest Farm. From the satellite cloud map, it appears like a soaring eagle, guarding the ecological security of North China.

Saihanba Mechanized Forest Farm
承德 塞罕坝机械林场

It is hard to imagine that more than half a century ago, this was a desolate and freezing land where "yellow sand obscured the sun and birds had no trees to settle on." For nearly 60 years, three generations of Saihanba people have kept their mission firmly in mind. They started this huge project from scratch, committed themselves to the undertaking of green development, and created the world's largest planted forest in an extremely harsh natural environment.

The word "Saihanba" stems from a combination of Mongolian and Chinese, meaning "a beautiful place with mountains and water resources". Historically, Saihanba was a natural wonderland with abundant water resources and dense forests. It was once an oasis and a royal hunting ground. However, later on, the excessive land reclamation and logging gradually turned it into an endless desert.

In order to change such a severe situation that the sandstorms were pressing on Beijing, China decided to establish a large-scale mechanized forest farm in the northern part of Hebei. In 1962, 127 college and university graduates from 18 provinces across China went to Saihanba, and together with 242 officials and workers of the forest farm, undertook the sacred mission of "blocking sandstorms for the capital and conserving water for Beijing and Tianjin".

The lowest temperature in Saihanba is minus 43.3°C and the annual average temperature is minus 1.3°C. Zhao Zhenyu, one of the first batch of forest builders, recalls, "At that time, there were sand dunes and barren mountains everywhere, and the wind blew hard with sand and snow grains covering the sky, hitting the face like a knife cut."

At that time, there was no shelter to keep these pioneers away from the harsh weather, and their living conditions were extremely difficult. Some of them lived in stables, some built shacks or dug cellars. In some cases, 20 people had to squeeze into one shack to sleep at night. They didn't have a door plank for their shack, so they had to use a straw mat as a substitute. At night, even wearing fur hats, they froze to the bone. In the morning, everywhere was covered with frost in the shack and even the bedding was frozen. For them, it would be a feast to eat black oat noodles and pickled vegetables and drink snow water.

Due to extremely harsh living conditions, coupled with the lack of experience in afforestation in high-altitude and cold regions, the survival rate of afforestation was less than 8% for two consecutive years in 1962 and 1963. The repeated failures of afforestation shook these pioneers' confidence. At this critical moment, four leaders of the forest farm, including Wang Shanghai, secretary of the Party Committee of the forest farm, moved their families here from other places with great determination, which soon strengthened these builders' confidence.

In the spring of 1964, the "Matikeng Battle" was launched, which had greatly boosted the morale of these pioneers. Due to the low temperature, the mud on their bodies froze into "ice armor", making a clanging sound as they walked, but no one complained. That year, they planted 516 mu of trees with a survival rate of over 90%. From then on, the afforestation cause in Saihanba was then put into full gear, developing from annual spring afforestation to spring and autumn afforestation. At its peak,

Saihanba in August
八月的塞罕坝

they planted over 2,000 mu of forest per day, and a total of 80,000 mu afforested in a year.

Today, the first generation of Saihanba pioneers are in their old years, but they have built a "green monument" with their ideals and beliefs, youth and passion, and the "Saihanba spirit" that they have created has been passed on to later generations across time and space.

Deng Baozhu, a second-generation pioneer who came to Saihanba in 1973, said that choosing forestry mean choosing dedication, and his two sons are now both in the forest farm, working as forest rangers and construction workers.

Yu Shitao, born in 1980 in Baoding, Hebei, plunged headlong into Saihanba right after graduating from university. "People working in forestry are usually unknown, because what they do won't show any result until 40 years later." He said, "We will hold on to the baton handed down by our predecessors and continue to forge ahead."

In 2008, Liu Jun and his wife Wang Juan came to the forest farm to work as watch-keepers on the "Wang Hai Tower" of the Moon Mountain at an altitude of 1900 meters. Back then, the "Wang Hai Tower" had no electricity, water or heating, and was devoid of people for six months during heavy snowfall. During important fire prevention periods, the couple would watch the forest within a radius of 20 kilometers every fifteen minutes and report to their superior every 15 minutes. They said, "we treat every tree like our own child." This is their working attitude.

It is difficult to start a business and even more difficult to maintain what has been achieved. Similarly, it's no easy task to guard this piece of hard-won forest, as it can be destroyed by simply a little spark or a moment of carelessness.

To ensure the safety of forest resources, the current Saihanba Forest Farm has established an integrated forest fire warning and monitoring system, which combines satellites, unmanned aerial vehicles, fire detection radars, video surveillance, mountain observations, and ground patrols to ensure a rapid response to any forest fire.

Since 1962, generations of people of Saihanba have responded to the call of the Party and used their blood, sweat, and lives to create the green miracle of turning a desert into an oasis, vividly interpreting the firm belief that "with lofty revolutionary ideals, we can overcome all difficulties" and the sense of mission and responsibility of being loyal to the cause of the Party and the people.

According to the assessment by the Chinese Academy of Forestry, the million-mu forests in Saihanba have built a strong green barrier, effectively blocking the southward invasion of the Hunshandake Sandland, conserving and purifying 284 million cubic meters of fresh water for the lower reaches of the Luanhe River and the Liaohe River every year, preventing soil erosion in the amount of 5.1355 million tons annually. It also sequesters 860,300 tons of carbon dioxide and releases 598,400 tons of oxygen each year.

With its excellent ecological environment and rich species resources, Saihanba has become a precious natural gene pool, with 261 species of terrestrial wild vertebrates, 32 species of fish, 660 species of insects, 179 species of macro fungi and 625 species of plants. It has become a "model of ecological civilization", a vivid interpretation of "lucid water and lush mountains are invaluable assets", and was awarded the "Earth Guardian Award" by the United Nations Environment Programme.

Nowadays, the natural scenery of Saihanba is vast and magnificent with profound historical connotation, unique Manchurian and Mongolian folk customs and abundant ecological tourism resources. It is reputed as "the source of rivers, the hometown of clouds, the world of flowers, and the ocean of forests", and has become one of the most famous ecological tourism scenic spots in North China, especially in the Beijing-Tianjin region.

 **Exercises**

Ⅰ. Comprehension

（1）Why is Saihanba known as the model of Chinese ecological civilization construction?

（2）Why was Chongli chosen as the ski resort of the Beijing Winter Olympics?

（3）What events did the Chinese team win gold medals in at the Beijing Winter Olympics?

（4）Apart from Yuefeng Canal, what other man-made canals are there in the Taihang Mountains?

Ⅱ. Translation

1. Term Translation

（1）北京冬奥会

（2）人定胜天

（3）脱贫攻坚，乡村振兴

（4）太行山精神

2. Passage Translation

在举世瞩目的北京冬奥会上，众多"第一次"被不断创造，高难度动作频频上演，年轻小将崭露头角，传奇老将续写传奇，竞争对手彼此关爱鼓励……一幕幕精彩瞬间，见证中国冰雪健儿自强不息、超越自我的拼搏历程，生动诠释了中华体育精神。赛场上，中国冰雪健儿以"使命在肩、奋斗有我"的责任担当，拼字当头，敢于拼搏、善于拼搏，取得了9金4银2铜的好成绩，践行了"人生能有几回搏"的铿锵誓言，创造了新的纪录，鼓舞和激励着中华儿女踔厉奋发、不懈奋斗。

Part Four
Hebei, the Birthplace of Many Outstanding Talents

As one of the birthplaces of the Chinese nation, Hebei Province is rich in natural resources and has many talented historical figures. Broad and grand, sophisticated and profound, Yan-Zhao Culture is deeply rooted and has a long history. In its long history, here emerged many famous historical figures, who have promoted and influenced the course of history, enriched the connotation of history, and become the cultural symbols and representatives of Hebei Province.

Here, many famous historical figures were once nurtured, such as King Wuling of the State of Zhao, Jing Ke, Xunzi, Dong Zhongshu and so on, who have been celebrated through the ages. They have not only deeply engraved on the land of Yan-Zhao the sense of righteousness and responsibility, such as being courageous in carrying out reforms, showing high respect for honor and justice, and being concerned about the country and the people, but have also shaped and influenced the spiritual temperament and value orientation of the whole Chinese nation.

Here, once emerged the so called "Yexia romance", which refers to a group of gifted and free-thinking scholars who gathered in Yecheng (today's Linzhang County, Handan, Hebei), the political center of Cao Cao's local government. They have become immortal figures in the history of Chinese literature. Here, once recorded the passion and vigour of the frontier fortress poems of the glorious age of the Tang Dynasty. And here, a large number of famous Yuan Drama writers were once nurtured and had been witnessed to go to the peak of Yuan Drama creation.

Lead-in Questions

(1) There were many great litterateurs and philosophers in ancient China. Do you know the ones that were born in Hebei?

(2) Many great literary works had been created in the history of ancient Chinese literature, such as the the Yuefu ballads of the Han Dynasty, the poetry of the Tang and Song Dynasties, the Yuan dramas, and the novels of the Ming and Qing Dynasties. Is there any of your favorite work from them? Please translation it into Chinese.

(3) Myths and legends are the earliest literature created by our ancestors. Do you know any myth or legend that originated from or was related to Hebei?

Jian'an Style

建安风骨

Chapter 19
The Poems and Songs

1. The Spread of "Ancient-oriented Poetics" and the "Mao Poetics"

The Book of Songs is the earliest collection of poems in China, and it has a very high status in the history of Chinese literature. This book was almost completely burnt during the campaign of "burning ancient books and burying scholars" launched by the First Emperor of Qin. When Emperor Wudi of the Han Dynasty implemented the policy of "deposing all the other schools of thought and only following Confucianism", only four schools of scholars annotated and taught *The Book of Songs*. They were Yuan Gu of Qi, Shen Pei of Lu, Han Ying of Yan, and Mao Chang of Zhao, and they were respectively known as "Qi poetics" "Lu poetics" "Han poetics" and "Mao poetics". Among them, the former three were modern-oriented poetics, which means they often related the social problems of their days to the explanation of The Book of Songs, but they gradually declined and died out after the Wei-Jin Period. "Mao poetics" was ancient-oriented, which means it mainly focused on the original meanings and teachings of *The Book of Songs*. In the Eastern Han Dynasty, Ma Rong wrote *Exegesis of Mao Poetics* (《毛诗诂训》), and Zheng Xuan worte annotations and commentaries on it, so "Mao poetics" thrived hereafter. After the Southern Song Dynasty, "Mao poetics" became the only school that survived. The original and essential information recorded in this book has important value to the study

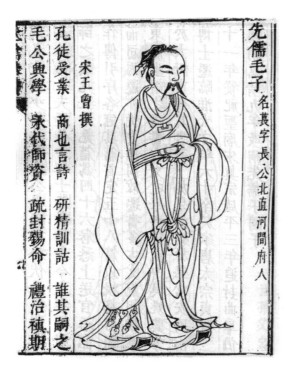

Mao Chang
毛苌

of *The Book of Songs* for later generations, and it has made important contributions to the poetry and literature of China and even the world. According to the legend, after Confucius revised *The Book of Songs*, it was passed down from Zi Xia, Zeng Shen, Meng Zhongzi, Gen Muzi, Xunzi, Mao Heng (commonly known as Senior Mao) to Mao Chang (commonly known as Junior Mao). In his early years, Mao Chang wandered about until he came to Chongdeli, Hejian Prefecture (today's Cangzhou City, Hebei). During the reign of Emperor Jing of the Han Dynasty, Liu De (with the posthumous title of "Xian", which means "dedication"), the head of the Hejian Vassal Kingdom, was keen on studying ancient Chinese culture. He set up a "Gentlemen Hall" in the north area of Hejian City to seek for scholars and sages. Mao Chang applied for a position there, and then started to give lectures on *The Book of Songs*. Today, there is a village called "Shijing Village" ("Shijing" is the Chinese pinyin for *The Book of Songs*) located on the Guyang River in Hejian City, which is the place where Mao Chang once taught and lived. To commemorate him, people of later generations built his cenotaph, the Mao Gong Ancestral Hall, and the Mao Gong Academy beside this village.

2. The Court Musician, Li Yannian

Li Yannian, born in Zhongshan (today's Dingzhou, Baoding, Hebei) in the Western Han Dynasty. He was a court musician during the reign of Emperor Wudi of the Han Dynasty. The Chinese idiom of "qing guo qing cheng (倾城倾国)", which means so beautiful a woman is, that her beauty is enough to cause the fall of a city or a country, first came from his song *The Beauty in the North*: "There is a beauty in the North,// Matchless and unique.// At the first sight (of the woman), the city crumbled,// And at the second sight, the entire country fell.// Even if to lose your city or country, don't lose the opportunity to get the beauty.// Once missed, it would be difficult to encounter the beauty again in this world." It is the earliest embryonic form of Chinese five-character-verse, which has enlightened later generations in the history of Chinese poetry.

3. Yuefu Ballads of the Han Dynasty and *Mulberry Tree of the Path* (《陌上桑》)

"Yuefu" was an government office set up since Emperor Wudi of the Han Dynasty to manage music affairs. It was also responsible for collecting folk songs from various places and accompanying them with music. Yuefu ballads are mainly collected in *Record of Art and Culture, History of Han Dynasty* (《汉书·艺文志》) and *The Collection of Yuefu Ballads* (《乐府诗集》) compiled by Guo Maoqian in the Song Dynasty. Many of the poems, according to the research, were created in such places as Handan, Hejian of Cangzhou and so on, such as *Chicken Crow* (《鸡鸣》) and *Meeting Xing* (《相逢行》, "Xing" is an ancient genre of poetry) collected in *Record of Art and Culture, History of Han Dynasty* and *Mulberry Tree of the Path* collected in *The Collection of Yuefu Ballads*. The masterpiece, *Mulberry Tree of the Path*, is a highly artistic five-character narrative poem, which is as popular as *The Ballad of Mulan* (《木兰辞》) that appeared later and *The Peacocks Flying Southeast* (《孔雀东南飞》). The famous lines of this poem are well known even to women and children, and are passed down from generation to generation. According to *Gu Jin Zhu* (《古今注》), a research note on all kinds of things of ancient and modern times) by Cui Bao, the poem is based on a real life story that happened in Handan, so it is the crystallization and sublimation of such life stories at that time.

4. "Jian'an Style" and Yexia Literati Group

At the end of the Eastern Han Dynasty, during the Jian'an Period and the early Wei and Jin Dynasties, the wars were frequent, the society was in great turbulence, and the people died in large numbers. But it is also a golden age of brilliant literature, during which a large number of talents emerged. During this period, Chinese literature entered an unprecedented prosperous and glorious era. The literary works created in this period have been highly praised by literary historians as "Jian'an literature" or "Jian'an style", which have the following characteristics: They have carried forward the realistic spirit of Yuefu ballads of the Han Dynasty; the main contents of these poems are the descriptions of the sufferings of common people and the up-lifting spirit of pursuing for achievements; the style is impassioned and sad, and the language is robust and bright. In particular, the new form of five-character-verse was widely adopted by the poets of that time, which pushed the five-character-verse poetry to the peak of its development. All these characteristics have exerted a profound influence on Chinese poetry. The representative figures of that time are Cao Cao and his two sons, Cao Zhi and Cao Pi, who are collectively known as the "Three Cao", as well as Kong Rong, Chen Lin, Wang Can, Xu Gan, Ruan Yu, Ying Yang and Liu Zhen, who are collectively called the "Seven Sages of Jian'an Period". During that time, Cao Cao and his sons had built up the capital city, Yedu, in Yecheng, which was the political center of Cao Cao's local government of Wei Prefecture in the Han Dynasty. There they built three famous buildings called Jinfeng, Tongque and Bingjing and attracted a lot of literati to carry out literary and political activities, so they were collectively called Yexia Literati Group by later generations.

5. Gao Shi and His Frontier Fortress Poems

From the early Tang Dynasty to the glorious age of the Tang Dynasty, many wars broke out on the borders, which led to the formation of the famous "school of frontier fortress poetry" in the poetic circles of the glorious age of the Tang Dynasty. The frontier fortress poems of that time had combined the characteristics of "Jian'an style" and the gorgeous features of the poems of the Qi Dynasty and the Liang Dynasty, presenting an impassioned and magnificent style and brimming with the high spirit

A Song of the Yan Country
《燕歌行》

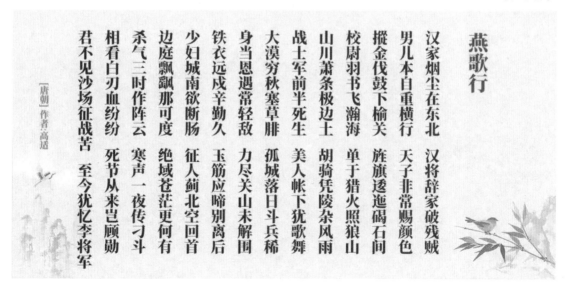

of the times. They not only have ideological and cognitive value, but also have a very high aesthetic taste. Among the large number of frontier fortress poets, Gao Shi, a native of Tiao County, Bohai Prefecture (today's Jing County, Hengshui City, Hebei), is one of the most famous poets, and he is honorably titled "Gao Cen" together with another poet, Cen Shen. Gao Shi had a great ambition, and he went to the border areas twice in his life, such as Liaoyang and Hexi, so he had a deep understanding of the life of the frontiers. His poems usually describe the magnificent scenery of the borders, the heroic ambition of soldiers galloping on the battlefields and fighting for great achievements, the patriotism of the soldiers bravely fighting against the enemies, the bitterness of the soldiers missing their wives, and the sacrifice and the hardship of the soldiers. His poems, such as *Under a Border-Fortress (Written to Music)* (《塞下曲》) and *A Song of the Yan Country* (《燕歌行》), are the representative works of the frontier fortress poems of the Tang Dynasty.

Chapter 20
The Yuan Dramas

During the Yuan Dynasty, Yuan Dramas became prosperous with their wide range of content and perfect artistic form due to many reasons, such as the ethnic conflicts, the social problems, the abnormal development of urban economy, the growing demand for popular culture and other reasons, especially the situation that the intellectuals were in low social status at that time, and they were familiar with the life of ordinary people, so they found an outlet for their talents in the creation of Yuan Dramas. Yuan Drama has become a wonderful art comparable to the poetry of the Tang Dynasty, the Ci of the Song Dynasty and the literary works of the Han Dynasty, and it is a unique literary form in the splendid history of Chinese literature and drama. At that time, Hebei, was the capital region of the Yuan Dynasty, and there emerged the leading figures of Guan Hanqing, Bai Pu, Ma Zhiyuan and Wang Shifu, who are collectively known as the "four masters

Guan Hanqing
关汉卿

121

of Yuan Drama", as well as Shang Zhongxian, Li Haogu, Ji Junxiang, Wang Heqing, Yang Guo, Liu Bingzhong, Lu Zhi, Zhu Lianxiu, Xianyu Biren and so on. They were engaged in the creation of Yuan Dramas, and some of them even directly participated in the performance, making the creation and performance of Yuan Dramas in Hebei take a leading position in the history of Chinese culture and drama.

Guan Hanqing was born in Puyin, Dadu (today's Anguo City, Baoding, Hebei) in the Yuan Dynasty. He is a great dramatist and is known as the founder of ancient Chinese drama. In 1958, he was listed as one of the world cultural celebrities. He created more than 60 Zaju works (Zaju, a kind of poetic drama set to music, flourishing in the Yuan Dynasty) with only 13 extant. And out of many of his Sanqu works (Sanqu is a type of verse popular in the Yuan Dynasty, including different kinds, such as Xiaoling, Taoqu, Canqu, etc.), only 57 Xiaoling, 13 Taoqu, and 4 Canqu are extant. He is the first of the "four masters of Yuan Drama", and his works have a great influence on his time and later generations. He was good at singing and dancing, and was proficient in the rhyme and rhythm of poetry. His representative works include *The Injustice Done to Dou E* (《窦娥冤》), *Attending a Conspiratorial Banquet only with a Machete*《单刀会》), *The Riverside Pavilion* (《望江亭》), *The Rescue of a Courtesan* (《救风尘》), *Butterfly Dream* (《蝴蝶梦》) and so on. They are still the repertoire of various opera performances today. Among them, *The Injustice Done to Dou E*, with the angry question of "Earth, if you can't tell the difference from the bad to the good, how can you be called earth?! Heaven, if you confuse the right and the wrong, how can you deserve your name as heaven!", is very touching and leaves the audiences with endless aftertastes.

Bai Pu was born in Zhending (today's Zhengding, Shijiazhuang, Hebei) in a troubled time of the late Southern Song Dynasty and grew up under the care of Yuan Haowen (a famous litterateur and historian). He showed outstanding talent since his childhood. He was very intelligent and read widely, and he was greatly accomplished in ancient classics and especially good at poetics. In his lifetime, he wrote 16 Zaju works, some existing Sanqu works including 4 Taoqu and 37 Xiaoling, and a book of Ci named *A Collection of Sounds of Nature* (《天籁集》). Some of his works eulogize the love between men and women, some sigh at the impermanence of life, and some describe the beautiful scenery of nature. His writing style is neat, graceful, unique, and brilliant, especially those works that eulogize the romantic love between men and woman. Those works are simple in language, but they are not frivolous or vulgar at all. They have a rich color of folk songs, and have won the praise of later generations. His most outstanding representative works handed down are *Over the Wall* (《裴少俊墙头马上》) and *Rain on the Plane Tree* (《唐明皇秋夜梧桐雨》). The former is one of the top ten classical comedies in China, while the latter tells the story of Emperor Xuanzong and Yang Guifei (an imperial concubine of the highest-ranking) of the Tang Dynasty. His poetic dramas, written in magnificent and gorgeous language, is regarded as the pioneer of the "school of literary grace" of the Yuan Dramas.

Ma Zhiyuan was born in Guangping (today's Yongnian District, Handan, Hebei) in the Yuan Dynasty. He wrote 15 Zaju works with 7 extant, and over 120 Xiaoling and Taoqu. His masterpiece, *Sorrow in the Han Palace* (《汉宫秋》), is one of the top ten classical tragedies in China, which tells about the story of Wang Zhaojun's going beyond the border to marry a Hun chieftain. "Whether in landscape description or in emotional expression, this work distinguishes itself as the second to none in Yuan Drama writing", commented by the critics of the Qing Dynasty. His Xiaoling, *Tune: Sunny Sand—Autumn Thoughts* (《天净沙·秋思》), goes like this: "Over old trees wreathed with rotten vines fly evening crows;// Under a small bridge near a cottage a stream flows;// On ancient road in the west wind a lean horse goes.// Westward declines the sun;// Far, far from home is the heartbroken one." (translated by Xu Yuanchong) It is a model of the Sanqu of the Yuan Dynasty, and it is regarded as "the ancestor of all the works on this theme".

Wang Shifu was born in Dingxing, Yizhou (today's Dingxing County, Baoding, Hebei) in the Yuan Dynasty. He wrote 14 Zaju works, of which 3 works are extant, and in 2 works only some fragments remain. His representative work, *Romance of the Western Chamber* (《西厢记》), is the most popular large-scale Yuan Zaju, which is far-reaching and well-known even to women and children. The line, "May all the lovers in this world can spend their lifetime with their beloved ones", is enlightening and soul-stirring, which boldly challenged the feudal ethics of thousands of years, and has been loved by many people for hundreds of years. Jia Zhongming, a drama critic of the late Yuan and early Ming dynasties, praised: "*Romance of the Western Chamber* is the best in the world." Cao Xueqin commented this work in his novel *A Dream of Red Mansions* (《红楼梦》) that, "Its words are enlightening and full of lingering artistic charm."

Shang Zhongxian was born in Zhending (today's Zhengding, Shijiazhuang, Hebei) in the Yuan Dynasty. He wrote 11 Zaju works with 3 extant, and some Sanqu works only with some fragments left. His representative work is *Liu Yi Delivers a Letter* (《柳毅传书》). He is good at depicting the feelings and personalities of the characters, and his language in this work is vivid and fresh. For example, in the Act One of this drama, there are such lines, "In the past, I swam in the waves,// And my hair was decorated with crystal combs.// But now, my clothes are ragged and my appearance is haggard.// Unlike other princesses with a happy marriage,// I became a shepherd by the Wuling River.// In the past, I had hoped my marriage to be harmonious and happy,// But now in the end I find my husband having eagle-like claws and python-like body.// He

Romance of the Western Chamber
《西厢记》

is manic and rude, and he speaks with no courtesy.// There is no hope for marital harmony.// He doesn't care about the relationship between husband and wife, just being furious toward me.// I don't care about his wealth,// And prefer to be alone and stay lonely." These lines vividly depict a sad shepherdess once growing up in the Dragon King's palace. Given such a vividly depicted image, it is no wonder that the author has been regarded as a master of Yuan Drama.

Li Haogu was born in Baoding (today's Baoding City, Hebei) in the Yuan Dynasty. He wrote 3 Zaju works: *Mighty Miracle God Splits Hua Mountain* (《巨灵神劈华岳》), *Zhao Taizu* (Taizu is a posthumous title for the first founder of a dynasty) *Quells the Haunted House* (《赵太祖镇凶宅》), and *Zhang Yu Boils the Sea* (《张生煮海》). All these works are myth dramas, of which only Zhang Yu Boils the Sea is extant. In the Ming Dynasty, Zhu Quan compared Li Haogu's works to be "the moon hanging on a solitary pine tree, delicate, graceful, bright and outstanding" in *Taihe Standard Music Score of Zaju* (《太和正音谱》). In the late Yuan and early Ming Dynasties, an excellent Zaju writer, Jia Zhongming, wrote an elegy for Li Haogu and commented on him, saying that he was a great writer and his works would make him immortal in the history.

Ji Junxiang was born in Dadu (today's Beijing) of the Yuan Dynasty. He created 6 Zaju works. The existing work, *The Zhao Orphan* (《赵氏孤儿》), is one of the top ten classical tragedies in China, and it is performed in various operas at home and abroad. Another existing work, *Chen Wentu Attains Enlightenment in a Dream in the Shade of a Pine Tree* (《陈文图悟道松阴梦》), is Sanqu with only one act left.

Wang Heqing was born in Daming of the Yuan Dynasty (in today's Handan). Tao Zongyi once commented on him in *Records in the South Village During the Slack Seasons* (《南村辍耕录》), saying that he was well known for his funny, frivolous, and unconstrained personality. He was a friend of Guan Hanqing, whom he once mocked and satirized. Of his works, 21 Xiaoling and 1 Taoqu are extant, which are collected in *Taiping Yuefu* (《太平乐府》), *White Snow in Sunny Spring* (《阳春白雪》), and *A Selection of the Masterpieces of Ci* (《词林摘艳》). His works have a strong color of slang and folk songs and a flavor of comic and juggling arts. He sharply satirized the world with a spicy, humorous, and mocking pen.

Chapter 21
The Prose and Miscellanea

1. Xun Kuang, the Father of Chinese Ci Fu, and the Highest Stage of the Pre-Qin Prose

Xun Kuang is an outstanding thinker and a great litterateur of the State of Zhao (today's Handan, Shijiazhuang, Hebei) in the Warring States Period, and he is also the last master of the Pre-Qin scholars. In terms of literature, he is not only a master of prose as famous as Mencius, but is also regarded together with Qu Yuan as the father of Chinese Ci Fu by later historians. His work *Xunzi* (《荀子》), including 32 articles, summarized and developed the philosophies of the Pre-Qin Period, which was unique in the "contention of a hundred schools of thought" at that time. His literary thought advocates simple and plain style and practicality, and opposes flashy style literature. The sentence that "The dye extracted from the indigo is bluer than the plant; so is the ice, which comes from water but colder than water" in the article of *Encouraging Learning* (《劝学》) has been well-known through the ages. *The Book of Fu* (《赋篇》), including five articles: *Rites* (《礼》), *Knowledge* (《知》), *Cloud* (《云》), *Silkworm* (《蚕》) and *Proverbs* (《箴》), is a collection of prose-style Fu. The term "Ci Fu" is the combination of the word "Ci", which is taken from Qu Yuan's *Chu Ci* (《楚辞》), and the word "Fu", which is taken from Xunzi's *The book of Fu*. Ban Gu, a great litterateur and historian of the Han Dynasty, once commented: "Xun Zi, the great scholar, and Qu Yuan, the official of the State of Chu, both suffering from slanderers and worrying about the future of the country, both wrote allegorical works of Fu, inheriting the tradition

Xun Kuang
荀况

of *The Book of Songs*". (from *Record of Art and Culture, History of Han Dynasty*), which illustrates Xunzi's position in the history of Chinese literature. One of his works, *Cheng Xiang* (《成相》), is a folk-style popular literature work accompanied by musical instruments, so some scholars also regard Xunzi as the founder of Chinese Tanci. (Tanci, one of Chinese folk art forms)

2. *Notes on the Book of Waterways* (《水经注》), a Book That Opened New Vistas

Li Daoyuan was a native of Zhuo County, Fanyang (today's Zhuozhou, Baoding, Hebei) of the Northern Wei Dynasty. He annotated the *Book of Waterways* written by an anonymous writer in the Wei and Jin Dynasties, and wrote the book, *Notes on the Book of* Waterways. It is a book that opened new vistas. The author had widely read many

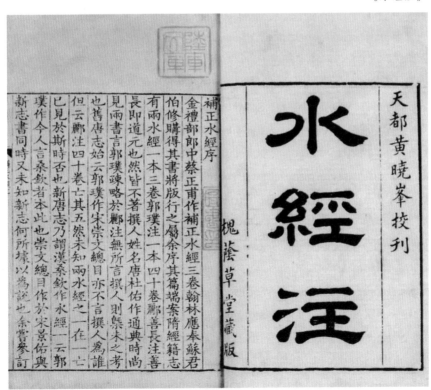

Notes on the Book of Waterways
《水经注》

books, collecting various kinds of information, such as the information about mountains, rivers, customs and practices, myths and legends, and historical anecdotes recorded in the documents since the Han and Wei Dynasties. Based on these materials and combined with his own experience of touring the Great Wall and the Yinshan Mountains with Emperor Wen of Northern Wei Dynasty, as well as the results of his field investigation of the rivers and the canals of the places where he had worked as an official, he wrote the book. In this book, in concise and beautiful words, he described the conditions of 1,200 rivers, such as their origins, the areas through which the rivers flew, the distributions of their branches, and the changes of the river courses since the ancient time. He also described the scenery of the beautiful rivers and mountains of the motherland, which shows his patriotism and his love for the people. *Notes on the Book of Waterways* is not only an outstanding geographical book, but also a fascinating prose collection of landscape travel notes written in concise and beautiful language. The careful and detailed descriptions of the landscapes show each landscape of its own unique features.

3. The Historical Document: *Records of the Temples of Luoyang* (《洛阳伽蓝记》), the Model of Parallel-style Prose

Yang Shanzhi was born in Peiping (today's Mancheng District, Baoding, Hebei) during the Southern and Northern Dynasties. His work, *Records of the Temples of Luoyang*, is a historical document of great literary value. Its language is beautiful, and the articles in it are written in a parallel-style mingled with Santi (Santi, a prose style free from parallelism), which is of distinctive characteristics. During the Northern Wei Dynasty, more than a thousand Buddhist temples were built in the capital city of Luoyang. These temples were splendidly decorated and extremely luxurious. Later, the temples were greatly destroyed in the wars. In the fifth year of Wuding Period (547 AD) under the reign of Emperor Xiaojing of the Eastern Wei Dynasty, Yang Shanzhi passed by Luoyang again, and he saw the city collapsed, the palaces overturned, the shrines reduced to ashes, and the temples ruined. For fear that the later generations might knew nothing about this, he wrote the book,

Records of the Temples of Luoyang (it consists of five volumes with each volume corresponding to an area, namely, the area within Luoyang City, the area out of the east gate of the city, the area out of the south gate of the city, the area out of the west gate of the city, and the area out of the north gate of the city), to record the rise and fall of the Buddhist temples and gardens. The book takes the rise and fall of the Buddhist temples as the main line, interspersed with the records of gardens, the stories of some famous people, and some anecdotes. Rich in content, it was written in a way of narration interspersed with comments, with the narrative parts mostly written in Santi and the descriptive parts often written in parallel-style prose. It can be regarded as an important geographical and historical work, as well as a precious and excellent prose work. Therefore, it is praised as the model of parallel-style prose of the Period of Wei, Jin and Southern and Northern Dynasties by later generations. Among all the articles, *Fayun Temple* (《法云寺》) and *Shouqiuli* (《寿丘里》) are the most famous.

4. *Pondering on an Ancient Battlefield* (《吊古战场文》), the Article That Enjoys the Reputation of "a Remarkable Piece of Writing in Thousands of Years"

Li Hua was born in Zanhuang (today's Zanhuang County, Shijiazhuang, Hebei) in the Tang Dynasty. He is a famous writer of ancient-style prose and one of the pioneers of the "ancient-style prose movement". During the Kaiyuan and Tianbao Periods of the Tang Dynasty, he was equally famous as Xiao Yingshi, a famous writer of Lanling (in today's Shandong Province). They both enjoyed the reputation that "in ancient times, Guan Zhong and Bao Shuya were praised by people, so are Xiao Yingshi and Li Hua nowadays. They correct any mistakes encountered, and make no remarks that are not based on ancient literature." Among the large number of various types of works written by Li Hua in his lifetime, such as Ji, Xu, Zhuan and Lun (Ji, Xu, Zhuan and Lun are types of writings of ancient Chinese), *Pondering on an Ancient Battlefield* can be called "a remarkable piece of writing in thousands of years". Firstly, the author started with the description of the battlefield scenery and took this part as the foreshadowing. Secondly, with his rich imagination, he described the tragic scene in the battlefield: the soldiers guarding the border, the fierce fighting in the battlefield, and the final destruction of the whole armies. Then the author changed the topic by reviewing the history full of frequent wars from the Warring States Period to the Han Dynasty. Finally, the author described the families of the dead holding memorial ceremonies, while "looking into the remote distance crying" and lamenting with the sighs of "Is this caused by the times, or by the fate? It has always been so since ancient times!" Written in verse combined with Santi, this article is sincere and sentimental, magnificent and powerful, mournful and touching, which has caused many writers of later generations to imitate, but few can match.

Chapter 22
The Ancient Novels and Legends

1. The Colorful Myths and Legends

Myths and legends are the earliest form of oral literature created by our ancestors. They are the foundation and the soil for Chinese literature, and have had a profound influence on the literature of the later generations. Almost all the iconic myths and legends of the Chinese nation originate from or are related to Hebei: The story that Pangu created heaven and earth originates from Qing County of Cangzhou, where locates the Pangu Temple; the story of Nüwa, who had melted stones to patch up the sky and created human beings by shaping people out of clay, comes from the southern foot of the Taihang Mountains, where remains Wa Huang's Palace (Nüwa is sometimes referred to respectfully as Wa Huang (娲皇), which translates literally as "Empress Wa"); the story of Fuxi, who created Bagua (the Eight Trigrams), originates from Xinle, Shijiazhuang, where remains the Fuxi Terrace; the legend of Lei Zu, the

Wa Huang's Palace
娲皇宫

wife of Huang Di (a legendary ruler, who is considered the ancestor of all Han Chinese in Chinese mythology), who first picked mulberry leaves and bred silkworms, is still circulating in Baoding; the story of Huang Di fighting against Chiyou (a famous tribal leader in ancient time) is still spreading in Zhuolu, Zhangjiakou; in Shunping of Baoding and Longyao of Xingtai, there are stories about the sage king Yao's handing over the crown to another trustworthy successor and thus starting a peaceful and prosperous era during the reign of the two sage kings of Yao and Shun; in Hengshui, there are stories about another sage king Yu, who is credited with taming the Yellow River's floods and dividing the empire into 9 provinces.

2. *The Annals of Natural History* (《博物志》), a Representative Work of Early Chinese Note-style Novel

The Annals of Natural History, written by Zhang Hua, a native of Fangcheng, Fanyang (today's Gu'an County, Langfang, Hebei) of the Western Jin Dynasty, is a fiction of supernatural tales, and a work imitating the style of *The Classic of Mountains and Rivers* (《山海经》). Originally it had 400 volumes, but later Emperor Wudi of the Jin Dynasty thought it was too lengthy and jumbled, so he ordered it to be deleted into 10 volumes. It is a representative work of the early Chinese note-style fiction, with its main content recording the strange things of exotic places and the daily news and events, mixed with some stories of immortals and Taoist magic arts. Although it is not regarded as one of the orthodox classics of Chinese culture, it is a preservation of Chinese ancient culture and an integral and organic part of Chinese culture. It is of great value to the study of ancient Chinese thought, mythology, culture and history. In particular, the records of oil and natural gas in northwest China are of great reference value. The articles, such as *Xue Tan Learns to Sing* (《薛谭学讴》) and *Taking a Raft* (《乘槎》), are excellent pieces and have been praised by later generations.

3. The Widely Circulated Fable Fiction, *The Wolf of Zhongshan* (《中山狼传》)

The fable fiction, *The Wolf of Zhongshan*, is written by Ma Zhongxi, a writer born in Gucheng (today's Hengshui City, Hebei) of the Ming

Statue of Cao Xueqin
曹雪芹塑像

Dynasty. It is a famous masterpiece in the history of Chinese literature, which shaped two typical artistic characters, Mr. Dongguo and a wolf. The story is set during the Warring States Period. King Jian of Zhao was hunting in Zhongshan, and there he came across a wolf. As the wolf fled desperately with the hunter in pursuit, it stumbled upon Mr. Dongguo and begged for shelter and finally won his pity. But once the crisis was over, the wolf showed its vicious nature and intended to eat Mr. Dongguo with no gratitude. While depicting the image of an insidious and ungrateful wolf, the work also shaped the image of Mr. Dong Guo, who is pedantic, coward, and excessively benevolent. It is an excellent work of moral significance, and soon after its publication, it was adapted into a Zaju. It has been widely circulated among the ordinary people and has great educational significance.

4. The Great Classic, *A Dream of Red Mansions*

As one of the four greatest ancient Chinese novels, *A Dream of Red Mansions* (originally named *The Story of the Stone* (《石头记》)), is written during the reign of Emperor Qianlong in the Qing Dynasty. It is generally believed that the ancestors of the author, Cao Xueqin, lived in today's Fengrun District of Tangshan, Hebei Province. Through the artistic sublimation of the rise and fall of a feudal family, the work gives a profound, exquisite and comprehensive description of the social life at that time, and strongly criticizes the feudal ethics, the ruling ideology, the imperial examination system, the arranged marriage and so on. It also reflects the author's fantasy of "patching up" the feudal system and the pessimistic mood of being unable to find a way out. The work is large in scale, precisely organized in structure, and beautiful and vivid in language. It is good at portraying characters, and shapes many artistic images with typical characters. It is of high ideological value and has achieved outstanding artistic achievement as the peak of realism in ancient Chinese novels. Its ideological and artistic beauty not only shocked the society at that time, but has also aroused continuous research enthusiasm of later generations, resulting in the emergence of "redology".

 # Exercises

Ⅰ. Comprehension

（1）Why were Yuan dramas born during the Yuan Dynasty?

（2）There is a "Shijing Village" in Hejian of Cangzhou. Who is it to commemorate?

（3）Among all the frontier fortress poets of the Tang Dynasty, which ones were related to Hebei? What are their representative works?

（4）In addition to the ancient writers introduced in this part, do you know any modern or contemporary celebrity that was born in Hebei? Please give some examples.

Ⅱ. Translation

1. Term Translation

（1）建安风骨

（2）《太阳照在桑干河上》

（3）笔力雄健，气魄宏大

（4）花间词派毛文锡

2. Passage Translation

《燕歌行》是唐代诗人高适的诗作。此诗概括一般的边塞战争，主要是揭露主将骄逸轻敌，不恤士卒，致使战事失利。全篇大致可分四段。首段八句写出师。其中前四句说战尘起于东北，将军奉命征讨，天子特赐光彩，已见得宠而骄，为后文轻敌伏笔；后四句接写出征阵容，旌旗如云，鼓角齐鸣，一路上浩浩荡荡，大模大样开赴战地，为失利时狼狈情景作反衬。第二段八句写战斗经过。其中前四句写战初敌人来势凶猛，唐军伤亡惨重；后四句说至晚已兵少力竭，不得解围。第三段八句写征人，思妇两地相望，重会无期。末段四句，前两句写战士在生还无望的处境下，已决心以身殉国；后两句诗人感慨，对战士的悲惨命运深寄同情。全诗气势畅达，笔力矫健，气氛悲壮淋漓，主旨深刻含蓄。

中文部分

第 1 篇
人文胜迹　文化遗产之美

　　河北是华夏文明的发祥地之一。河北大地上的先民，创造了灿烂文明，留下宝贵、丰厚的历史文化遗产。

　　河北省是文物大省，省级以上文物保护单位达 963 处，其中全国重点文物保护单位达 287 处。拥有长城（山海关、金山岭）、避暑山庄及周围寺庙、清东陵清西陵、大运河（衡水市景县华家口夯土险工、沧州市东光谢家坝，以及南运河沧州—衡水—德州段 94 公里遗产段）等 4 项世界文化遗产。此外，娲皇宫、隆兴寺、苍岩山、赵州桥、满城汉墓等文化遗产充分展现了河北深厚的文化积淀，反映了河北人民勤劳智慧的精神面貌。河北，这片文化的热土，在新世纪正发出璀璨的光芒。

　　截至 2022 年 12 月底，河北在全国可移动文物普查平台登录可移动文物 322 610 件 / 套，实际数量 1 402 448 件。其中，珍贵文物 60 109 件 / 套，包括一级文物 1 313 件 / 套。

　　当我们走近其中，尤其是河北的 18 件国宝级文物，更能领略这片土地上孕育传承的人文根脉，感受到历史深处射来的中华文明的光亮。

第1章
河北境内的长城
——雄奇壮美留燕赵

河北最具代表性的人文符号，当属长城。

在中国长城历史上，河北省有着十分特殊的地位，从战国时期到明代，基本上各个朝代的长城在河北都有遗址，这在中国众多省份中是极为少有的。

河北现存长城 2 498.5 千米，行经 9 市 59 个县（市、区），长城资源数量居全国第 2 位。全国长城保存最完整、建筑最雄伟、文化最丰富的地段，均在河北。[①]

在山海之间 8 千米构筑修建的山海关，是明长城关隘系统的代表；金山岭长城在建筑构件、形制上完美保存了长城原貌；张家口则因现存长城多代建筑、分布广泛、形制丰富，被称为"历代长城博物馆"……除了长城本体，河北长城沿线还有丰富的历史资源、生态资源和文化资源。

长城拥抱大海，穿越燕山，在燕赵大地上见证了中国 2 000 多年的历史。如今在河北境内留存着大约 2 500 千米长城，绵亘于燕山与太行山的山峦之中：一条自东向西，从渤海边的山海关老龙头，经秦皇岛、唐山、承德、天津、北京、张家口与山西的长城相接，横贯河北北部燕山山脉；另一条自北向南，从北京的慕田峪起始，经北京、张家口、保定、石家庄、邢台至邯郸武安，纵贯河北西部太行山山岭。在这两条线路中包含着万里长城中最雄伟、保存最完整、文化最丰富的精华地段。

《史记·赵世家》记载：公元前 369 年，中山国筑长城。在燕、赵两大强国之间求生存，中山国全力自保，在今天保定市境内修建了一道不足 90 千米的长城，这是河北境内已知修筑年代最早的长城。

春秋战国时期，北部诸侯国与游牧民族比邻而居，游牧军队飘忽不定的行踪和迅疾猛烈的攻击，让中原诸国无从招架，于是燕、赵等国开始用长墙将烽火台连接，以期阻挡北方民族的马蹄，出于划分边界与保护自己的需要，各诸侯国之间也筑起了一道道长墙。

从秦代到明代，2 000 多年间 20 多个朝代都曾大规模修筑长城。在京津冀地区，历

---

① 《中国长城保护报告》，国家文物局 2016 年 11 月。

代长城总是修筑在自然气候与地理环境的分界带上，基本与 400 毫米等降水量线一致。巧合的背后其实是自然选择，在这一地区，长城的南侧是以种植业为主半干旱地区，植被多为林地草原；北侧则是以牧业生产为主的干旱地区，被草原和荒漠所覆盖。

河北，横跨农牧两大地理环境。特殊的地理环境，造就了农耕与游牧两种民族轮番上演和平与纷争、繁荣与衰落。于是，长城选择了河北，在一砖一石的堆砌中，筑成了最坚固最精彩的一段。

公元前 221 年，秦始皇统一中国，为防范北方草原势力的南下，他将燕、赵、秦三国的旧长城修缮连接，并修建新的长城。公元前 214 年，一条西起陇西、东至辽东的长城完工，这是第一条名副其实的万里长城。河北境内的秦长城，大部分存留在张家口与承德北部一带，长度超过 460 千米，在历代改扩建与岁月的洗礼中，秦长城多数已湮没在历史的尘埃里。

打通河西走廊的汉代，修成了一条西起大宛^①贰师城，东至黑龙江北岸，全长近 10 000 千米的长城。古丝绸之路有一半路程沿着长城而行。汉长城有 250 多千米经过张家口与承德。在张家口的尚义县，仍有清晰可辨的汉长城遗址，夯土的城墙随着山势起伏，烽火台兀立于山势险峻之处，静默凝重，依稀可以窥见汉长城的雄伟。

1368 年，明朝建立，元朝统治者被迫退回北部草原。不甘失败的蒙古大军，始终怀有再次南下的梦想。面对北方强敌的觊觎，1421 年，明成祖朱棣将都城从南京迁至北京。为了长治久安，明朝廷开始修筑边墙，边墙就是明长城。

我们今天看到的长城，绝大部分是修建于 14 世纪的明朝。西起嘉峪关，东至鸭绿江的明长城总长约 6 300 千米，设置了都司、卫、所等不同级别的军事组织机构，是历朝历代中修筑时间最长、规模最大、质量最高、建筑也最为精美的长城。它在北方的山脊间，划出一条与蒙古部族的分界线，是大明王朝最北的防线。

中国古代军事家一直遵循着一条防御原则——因险设塞——以便用较少的兵力抵御较多的敌人。这一点在明长城的选址上得到完美体现，即最大限度地利用山形地势，有的要塞设置在山巅锁住峪口，有的隐匿在深谷封住咽喉。这种选择意外地成就了明长城的长城美学，长墙城楼与山川地形完美契合，线条绝美；各色建筑与山川植被互为依托，气势磅礴。

长城的雄、险、奇、长，即便在岁月中坍塌残缺，也有一种壮志难酬的悲壮美。长城之所以伟大，还在于它所拥有的精妙且富有创造性的建筑。边墙与长城这两个称呼都不能概括它的全部，它是由关隘、城墙、敌楼、烽火台、营城等诸多工事组成的完整防御体系。

1568 年，明朝抗倭名将戚继光调任蓟镇总兵，管辖蓟镇境内 1 500 余里长城。在随后的 16 年间，战神戚继光以长城总设计师的新身份，翻修改造出明长城最精华的一段。

① 大宛（dà yuān），古代中亚国名，中国汉代时，泛指在中亚费尔干纳盆地附近各个国家和居民，大宛国大概在今费尔干纳盆地。

给旧长城包上青砖是戚继光的一大创举，砖包墙的工艺并没有改变长城的形态，却让它的坚固性得以提升。戚继光将他的代表作，经浙江台州试验行之有效的空心敌楼，在金山岭发扬光大走向极致。全长 10.5 千米的金山岭，设有空心敌楼 67 座，最远间隔 200 多米，最近不足 50 米，是明长城空心敌楼最为密集多样的一段，一旦迎敌，相望相助，构成一道严密的防御体系。

万里长城宛如一条巨龙，跨过浩瀚的沙漠，穿过茫茫的草原，翻过巍巍的群山，随之引颈入海。这入海的部分便是河北明长城的东部起点——老龙头。

在辽西走廊的最西端，渤海与角山构成天然屏障，山海之间仅有 8 千米的距离。这里咽喉锁钥，自古就是华北通向东北的要冲，距离北京 280 千米，两地之间多是利于骑兵冲杀的平原，它的存亡关乎京师的安危。明初在这里设置卫所，从明朝中后期开始，雄踞于此的山海关逐渐赢得了"天下第一关"的称号。

长城，虽名为城，与城市的城墙相比，长城的姿态更为开放，在大多数岁月里，成千上万的关口不是为了阻拦，而是为了交流。历史上，长城是中原王朝与周边民族攻防

潘家口水下长城

的前线，而在更漫长的和平年代，它是象征着秩序与约束的边贸口岸，南北的物产、文化在这里交换。伴随着长城的除了荒原，还有大量的城镇，赤峰、秦皇岛、张家口、大同、榆林、固原、银川、兰州、武威、张掖、酒泉、嘉峪关、敦煌……这些城市的缘起与繁荣离不开长城，受惠于边境的关市与马市贸易。以防御为主建立起来的长城，在更为广阔的空间里，却是以民族间贸易与融合平台的形象示人。

2 000 多年间，人类记忆在长城不断叠加，令冰冷的城墙也变得温暖。

但无论是对筑长城、守长城甚至是游长城的人来说，它都象征了这个国家的底线不可逾越，体现了这个民族的力量、智慧与决心。长城，虽然以防御姿态出现，但在中国人的眼中更多的却是一种象征。对于一个国家来说险关要塞不可或缺，但众志成城不屈不挠更为重要，这是长城独有的坚强意志和伟大力量，这种意志和力量曾拯救中华民族于水火之中，凝聚起了全民族救亡图存的决心与必胜的力量。

第 2 章
避暑山庄及周围寺庙
——万里车书皆属国

在河北最北端与内蒙古交界的地方，有一片世界上最大的人工林海，这就是塞罕坝。300多年前，这里曾经是清朝康熙帝圈定的木兰围场，每年秋天，康熙帝亲率大军，与北方的蒙古王公一同狩猎、驰骋比武、分旗封王、经济援助，数万骁勇善战的将士逐鹿草原，

雪后普陀宗乘之庙

避暑山庄湖区

史称木兰秋狝（xiǎn）①。这既是一年一度的军事演习，也是清王朝与北方民族结盟的盛会。木兰秋狝可谓是康熙帝巩固统一大业的一大谋略，而为了让这道塞上雄藩永固百年，康熙帝谋划了一个更为庞大的体系，木兰秋狝的必经之地热河纳入了他的视野。热河，位于蒙古高原进入中原大地上的一条要道上，距北京约180千米，朝发夕至，往还无过两日。在热河建造一座行宫，向东可连通东北，向北可沟通蒙古，向西北可联络蒙回各部，向南可控制中原。于是，修避暑山庄，建外八庙。在热河，帝王宫苑与皇家寺庙相辉映，开创了民族团结与文化交融的典范。

1703年，康熙帝开始设计和指挥行宫的建造。1713年，行宫初步建成。清雍正帝继位之后，取"承受先祖德泽"之意，将热河改名为承德，而他的继任者乾隆帝，又在康熙帝布局避暑山庄的基础之上，增设宫殿和大型园林设施，移南方胜景入北园，使避暑山庄有了南秀北雄的兼美之意，遂成避暑山庄"七十二景"。

总面积5.64平方千米的避暑山庄，集中国古代造园艺术和建筑艺术之大成，是世界现存最大的古典皇家园林，分为宫殿区、湖泊区、草原区和山景区四大部分，从西北部最高峰到东南部湖沼、草原地带，相对等差180米，整体上表现出一种四方朝揖、众向所归的气势。

宫殿区位于湖泊南岸，地形平坦，占地1平方千米，是清朝皇帝理朝听政、举行大典和寝居之所，由正宫、松鹤斋、万壑松风和东宫四组建筑组成。正宫是宫殿区的主体

---

① 古代君王一年出猎四次，分别是春蒐、夏苗、秋狝、冬狩。"木兰"为满语，意为哨鹿，是满族人的一种狩猎方式。清代皇帝为了沿袭骑马射猎的传统，秋季前往木兰围场进行哨鹿，称之为木兰秋狝。

建筑，包括九进院落，分为"前朝""后寝"两部分。主殿叫"澹泊敬诚"殿，用珍贵的楠木建成，因此也叫楠木殿，建筑风格朴素淡雅，但不失帝王宫殿的庄严。湖泊区在宫殿区的北面，湖泊面积包括洲岛约占4.3平方千米，有8个小岛屿，将湖面分割成大小不同的区域，层次分明，洲岛错落，碧波荡漾，富有江南鱼米之乡的特色。山景区在山庄的西北部，面积约占全园的五分之四，这里山峦起伏，沟壑纵横，众多楼堂殿阁、寺庙点缀其间。草原区在湖区北面的山脚下，地势开阔，有万树园和试马埭（dài），呈现出一派碧草茵茵、林木茂盛的茫茫草原风光。

避暑山庄，这座皇家园林，以其独特的地形地貌特征为选址和总体设计的依据，完全依赖自然地势，因山就水，顺其自然。它融合了南北建筑艺术的精华，既有南方园林的风格、结构和工程做法，又沿袭了北方常用的手法，成为南北建筑艺术完美结合的典范。与京城故宫的黄瓦红墙，描金彩绘，堂皇耀目形成鲜明对比，山庄内的建筑规模适中，多采用青砖灰瓦、原木本色、淡雅庄重，简朴适度。严谨的宫殿布局、朴素的建筑风格、自然的野趣，使宫殿与天然景观和谐地融为一体，达到了回归自然的境界。这是中国园林史上的一个辉煌里程碑，是中国古典园林艺术的杰作，享有"中国地理形貌之缩影"和"中国古典园林之最高范例"的盛誉。

康乾年间，清廷先后在承德避暑山庄东面和北面的山麓，依山势起伏而建十二座金碧辉煌、规模宏伟、风格迥异的皇家寺庙，这些庙宇融汇中国汉、藏、蒙等多民族建筑艺术的精华，按照建筑风格分为藏式寺庙、汉式寺庙和汉藏结合式寺庙三种，与青砖灰瓦、古朴典雅的避暑山庄形成鲜明的对比，是中国现存最大的皇家寺庙群。这十二座寺

普宁寺

庙在避暑山庄北部、东北部的山丘地带有八座，自西向东依次是罗汉堂、广安寺（已毁）、殊像寺、普陀宗乘之庙、须弥福寿之庙、普宁寺、普佑寺、广缘寺；在避暑山庄以东的武烈河东岸有四座，自北向南依次是安远庙、普乐寺、溥仁寺、溥善寺（已毁）。当年罗汉堂、广安寺、普乐寺由内务府管理，其余有八座寺庙（实际是九座寺庙，其中普佑寺附属于普宁寺），由清政府理藩院管理，由于都在古北口外，故统称"外八庙"。久而久之，外八庙便成了这十二座寺庙的代称。外八庙以汉式宫殿建筑为基调，吸收了蒙、藏、维等民族建筑艺术特征，创造了中国的多样统一的寺庙建筑风格。这些寺庙主要是西方、北方少数民族的上层及贵族在朝觐见皇帝的时候礼佛之用。外八庙像一颗颗星星环避暑山庄而建，呈烘云托月之势，构筑起了中国最为雄伟集中的寺庙群。避暑山庄及其周围寺庙，创造性地解决了中国历史上民族分裂的难解之结，促进了中华民族的大融合，开创了民族团结与文化交融的典范。这里上演着一幕幕促进各民族守望相助和睦共生的感人故事，随着史册，流传至今。

第3章
清东陵与清西陵
——清代帝王的归宿

在长达几千年的中国封建社会，作为王朝最高的统治者，很多皇帝自登上龙位就开始营建自己的陵墓。地面是现世的权威，地下则是永生的梦想。在他们看来，死后也要和生前一样，归身之地与现实居所同等重要，他们的丧葬之事自然采用国家的最高礼制来办理。

于是，皇陵这种特殊的建筑，往往凝结了中国人民巧夺天工的艺术才能，收藏着人类文化的瑰宝，体现了当时最高水平的规划思想，集中了那个时代建筑技术和艺术的辉煌成就。明清是中国陵寝修建史上的集大成时期，将中国古代陵寝的营建推向高峰。

遵化清东陵局部图

清代皇家陵寝是清朝皇帝悉心规划营建的墓葬建筑，体现了中国封建社会的最高丧葬制度和千百年封建社会的宇宙观、生死观、道德观和习俗，也体现了当时中国最高水准的规划思想和建筑艺术。清代皇室共有 3 处陵寝，分别在辽宁沈阳，称北陵；河北唐山遵化，称东陵；河北保定易县，称西陵。清东陵的营建早于清西陵，历时 247 个寒暑，是中国现存规模最为宏大，体系最为完整，保存最为完好的帝王陵墓建筑群。

清东陵位于河北省遵化市马兰峪西部昌瑞山主峰南麓，占地 78 平方千米。整个陵区共有 5 座清帝陵：孝陵（顺治）、景陵（康熙）、裕陵（乾隆）、定陵（咸丰）、慧陵（同治），4 座后陵，5 座妃园寝，1 座公主陵。

联合国世界遗产专家评价清东陵是"人类具有创造性的天才杰作"。

整个陵区，北以昌瑞山做后靠如锦屏翠帐，南有金星山做前朝如持笏朝揖，中间有影壁山做书案可凭可依，东有鹰飞倒仰山如青龙盘卧，西有黄花山似白虎盘踞，东西两条大河如玉带环绕。群山环抱的堂局辽阔坦荡，雍容不迫，可谓地臻全美、景物天成。

陵区以昌瑞山主峰下的孝陵为中轴线，依山势呈扇形东西排列，主次分明，尊卑有序。

各陵都按规制营建了一系列建筑，总体布局为"前朝后寝"。"百尺为形，千尺为势"的审美思想贯穿于每一座陵寝建筑中，使各单体建筑达到了近乎完美的空间组合。远望时，殿宇、城垣、门坊、道路、桥涵，金黄碧绿，丹红雪白，气势恢宏壮丽而深沉。由远及近，步移景易，变化丰富，秩序严谨，相得相济，引人入胜，是中国古代陵寝的典范之作，其建筑艺术达到了中国建筑的顶峰。

清东陵是中国历代皇陵的集大成者，是中国古代劳动人民智慧的结晶，综合体现了中国传统的风水学、建筑学、美学、哲学、景观学、丧葬祭祀文化、宗教、民俗文化等文化元素，具有重要的历史价值、艺术价值和科学价值。

清室从雍正帝起实行祖孙同葬、父子不同眠。清西陵由此开始建造。

清西陵位于河北易县城西 15 千米处的永宁山下，周界约 100 千米，面积约 800 平方千米，共有清帝陵 4 座：泰陵（雍正）、昌陵（嘉庆）、穆陵（道光）、崇陵（光绪），后陵 3 座，王爷、公主、妃子园陵 7 座。

清西陵北依峰峦叠翠的永宁山，南傍蜿蜒流淌的易水河，古木参天，景态雄伟。从雍正帝选址建陵开始，清王朝就在永宁山下、易水河畔、陵寝内外种植了数以万计的松树，现在这里有古松树 1.5 万余株、青松幼柏 20 余万株，陵区内松柏葱郁，山清水秀，14 座陵寝掩映在华北地区最大的人工古松林之中，若隐若现，俨然一副绚丽的山水画。陵区千余间宫殿建筑和百余座古建筑、古雕刻气势磅礴。每座陵寝严格遵循清代皇帝建陵制度，皇帝陵、皇后陵、王爷陵均采用黄色琉璃瓦盖顶，妃、公主、阿哥园寝均采用绿色琉璃瓦盖顶，这些不同的建筑形制，体现出不同的景观和风格。

泰陵是清西陵的首陵，位于永宁山的主峰之下，埋葬着雍正及他的皇后孝敬、皇贵妃敦肃，规模宏大，体系完整。以泰陵为中心，其他各陵分布在东西两侧，规制与清东陵基本相同。

昌陵位于泰陵西侧，建筑形式与泰陵基本相同，规模并列。穆陵和崇陵相对规模较小。

清西陵体现了中国历代帝王陵寝的最高水准，更是一部精美的艺术杰作，座座陵寝都反映出清朝的历史文化、建筑文化、生态文化和风水文化，成为自然环境与陵寝建筑相结合的最伟大案例。

易县 清西陵　泰陵

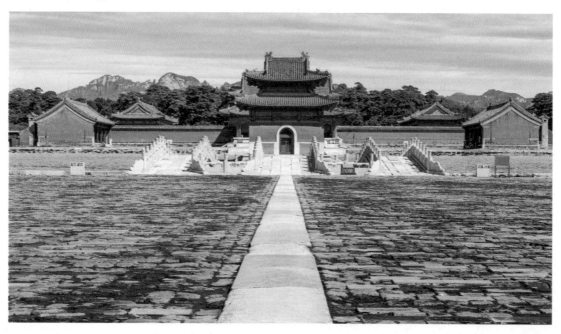

第4章
河北境内的大运河
——千里舳舻，水运南北

这是地球上对自然地理面貌改变最大的人类工程，她在主要大江大河皆东流的神州大地上，以连接南北的姿态跨越地球十多个纬度，联通海河、黄河、淮河、长江、钱塘江五大自然水系。中国人将智慧、勇气、决心倾注在3 200千米的河道上，与大自然共同刻画出这一奇观。

如果说长城是凝固的历史，那么大运河就是流动的文化。一部运河史，半部中华文明史。在大运河上流淌的不仅是各类漕运粮船，也沟通了南北的文化交流。

这是一首永不止歇的大地史诗，从公元前5世纪开始书写，6 000里的大运河沿岸催生出一座座文化名城，承载着无数繁华盛景，沉淀着无数兴衰的记忆。作为世界

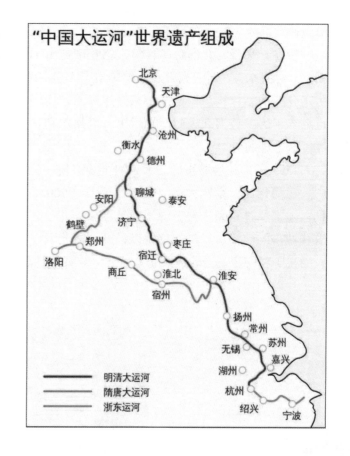

上建造时间最早、使用最久、空间跨度最大的人工运河，除了人们熟知的京杭大运河，还包括浙东运河和隋唐运河，这个伟大工程有六分之一流经河北。

河北境内的大运河，全长530多千米，流经廊坊、沧州、衡水、邢台、邯郸等地，分为北运河、南运河、卫运河和卫河四大河段。

蜿蜒流淌的大运河在空间上横跨530多千米，而在建造时间上却跨越了1 800多年。

从 204 年开始，曹操建邺都（今河北邯郸临漳县西南），筑冰井台、铜雀台、金虎台，从此邺城成为中国北方政治、经济中心，不仅留下了建安文学的辉煌，也为北方运河大规模的开凿书写了肇始的篇章。

为了北驱乌桓一统天下，曹操先后开凿白沟、利漕渠、平虏渠、泉州渠和新河五条人工漕运河渠，把华北大平原上的滹沱河、漳水、古易水、潞水等水系相互贯通，成为他统一北方的漕运利器。

608 年，隋炀帝杨广征集河北诸郡百余万人开凿永济渠，自洛阳向北经河北与北京相连。

1271 年，元世祖忽必烈定都大都（今天的北京），自此，北京这座城市成为影响后世近千年的国家政治中心。1276 年，元军攻克南宋都城临安（今杭州）。此时，承担着都城运输与供水生命线的大运河已经无需绕道洛阳。如何裁弯取直，让运河从富庶的江南直达大都成为横亘在元朝统治者面前的新难题。

最终，来自河北邢台的科学家郭守敬提出了解决方案。他花费了数年时间进行地形勘察，寻找水源，计算落差，并绘制出了大运河裁弯取直的线路图。他提出了大运河"弃弓走弦"的整体构想，即在山东修建运河，连接河北和江苏，实现京杭直航。这份设想也融入了另一位河北人的辛勤付出，沧州水利学家马之贞陪同郭守敬勘查河道，共同解决了这个难题。

1293 年，裁弯取直后的大运河全线通航，运河的涟漪汇聚成更为广阔的水系。与隋唐大运河相比，京杭大运河航道缩短了约 900 千米，从此，南方的粮食、其他物资和大量人才都经过这条水路源源不断地汇聚到北京，南北物资进出京，都要经过河北。河北沿线城市的政治、经济地位得以提升。河北可以直接与富庶的江南开展贸易往来，河北人的视野和脚步也沿着运河北上南下，继而出海走向世界。

河流与城市，大多相辅相成，彼此成就，相得益彰，著名的城市一般与河流相伴而生，很难想象一座城市能离开淡水的佑助而能繁盛兴旺。中国大运河孕育着一座座沿河城镇，它们萌兴、发展和壮大。

郑口、泊头和沧州就是大运河河北段三座典型的运河城镇。他们用各自的发展史，勾勒出一幅大运河沿线城市的发展、进化图谱。

沧州便是其中的佼佼者。

沧州有 1 500 余年建州史，是一座因运河而兴的城市。宋末元初的时候，沧州运河沿岸经济繁荣，有"小燕京"之称。作为沧州的母亲河，大运河在这里流经 8 县（市、区），绵延 215 公里，沿途遗迹分布众多，河道保存完好，最能代表北方运河原真性。沧州也是在京杭大运河贯穿的所有城市里里程最长的城市。

2014 年 6 月 22 日，中国大运河申遗成功，大运河河北段的"两点一段"——衡水市景县华家口夯土险工、沧州市东光县连镇镇谢家坝，以及南运河沧州—衡水—德州段 94 千米遗产段，被定为世界文化遗产点（段）。这是河北省拥有的第四处世界文化遗产。

随着大运河申遗成功，大运河沿岸的古码头、古城镇、古村落也逐渐被挖掘出来，越来越多的人开始行走大运河河北段，各个沿河城市也开始重温运河历史，挖掘运河文化。

运河，是应航运的需求而生。随着人类工业文明的发展，进入到 20 世纪六七十年代，公路、铁路等陆路交通迅猛发展，沟通南北舟楫相连的大运河航运，就只停留在老一辈人的记忆之中了。

因为大运河的河道、河堤还在，现在的大运河还在发挥着一个重要功能——南水北调东线输水。

2022 年 4 月 28 日，位于山东德州的四女寺枢纽南运河节制闸开启，与此同时，位于天津市静海区的九宣闸枢纽南运河节制闸开启，南水北调之水经南运河与天津本地水汇合。至此，京杭大运河实现近一个世纪以来首次全线通水。输水，将成为大运河今后很长一段时间内的重要功能，千年大运河将再次焕发出勃勃生机。

第5章
河北大地上的古塔

河北是古塔众多的省份。

河北多古塔，与河北佛教传播早有关。

魏晋南北朝时期，佛教在中国广泛传播。北朝时期，河北就开始佛寺、佛塔的营造修筑。到了唐代，河北是长安沟通东北的重要通道，佛教在河北也进一步兴盛。河北佛塔大放异彩，是在宋辽金时期。

根据 2013 年河北省对古塔进行的一次统计，河北现存古塔 230 余座，数量上在全国能列入前五，其中全国重点文物保护单位就有 30 多座。石家庄、保定、邯郸、张家口、承德等地古塔均在 30 座以上。河北古塔数量多、品质高、类型丰富，且不乏存世孤品。本章选取了河北省的 5 座代表性古塔，在木瓦砖石间探寻它们的前世今生之美。

1. 河北定州开元寺塔

始建于 1001 年的河北定州开元寺塔，共十三层，高 83.7 米，是我国现存最高的砖塔，1961 年被国务院列为第一批全国重点文物保护单位。

定州开元寺塔

荆轲塔局部

据文献记载，北宋初年，定州开元寺僧会能往西天竺（印度）取经，得佛教中传说的舍利子而回。宋真宗咸平四年（1001 年），宋真宗下诏，命在定州开元寺内建塔纪念，到宋仁宗至和二年（1055 年）建成此塔（一说此塔是在宋仁宗皇祐四年即 1052 年建成）。这座因佛教意义出现、耗时 50 多年建成的高塔，却由于所处的特殊历史时期和特殊地理位置，很快就被赋予了更多的军事意义。宋王朝为了防御北部辽国的侵扰，常利用此塔瞭望敌情。

2. 河北易县荆轲塔

荆轲塔现塔高 24 米，为八角十三层实心砖塔，造型古朴。下有莲花仰托，上有舍利子封顶，塔身每层高度递减，整座塔显得挺拔俊秀。塔每层之八隅均悬风铃，经风吹动，清脆悦耳，音传四野。

荆轲塔又称圣塔院塔，位于河北省保定市易县县城西南 2 千米处的荆轲山上，于 2006 年被国务院列为第六批全国重点文物保护单位。众所周知，"慷慨悲歌"一直是燕赵整体文化概念最鲜明的风格标签，而荆轲无疑被视为推动这一风格形成的代表性人物。荆轲塔的由来便可追溯至公元前 227 年，荆轲在易水河畔辞别燕太子丹等人西行刺秦王的义举。史料记载，当年燕太子丹曾在荆轲山为荆轲建馆舍，易水一别后，荆轲的衣冠冢也建在这里。辽乾统三年（1103 年），荆轲衣冠冢上建起了圣塔和寺院。明万历年间，改圣塔寺为圣塔院，之后历朝历代皆有重建修葺。

正定天宁寺凌霄塔

正定开元寺须弥塔

正定广惠寺华塔

3. 河北正定天宁寺凌霄塔

凌霄塔始建于唐代，塔高 40.98 米，为一座砖木混合平面呈八角形的楼阁式塔，上下共九层，下三层塔身为砖砌，四至九层为木构。塔的砖砌部分在宋代重修，其上木构各层为金代重建。

凌霄塔最独特之处，是塔内部"塔心柱"的结构设计，国内仅存一例。凌霄塔塔身第四层中心部位立有一根直达塔顶的塔心柱。塔心柱在每层通过水平方向放射而出八根梁与塔身的八角相连接，使塔心柱、四至九层抱柱、四至九层转角铺作与梁上下左右构成一个稳固的整体，同时承载与分散了九层塔顶与塔刹的负荷。

值得一提的是，正定是河北省唯一保留 4 座千

正定广惠寺华塔细节

正定临济寺澄灵塔

衡水市景县景州塔

年以上古塔的历史名城。天宁寺凌霄塔与开元寺须弥塔、临济寺澄灵塔、广惠寺华塔并称"正定四塔"，历经千年，始终巍然耸立。正定古塔的密集是河北省古塔整体规模的一个缩影。

4. 河北景县景州塔

景州塔位于河北省衡水市景县，原名释迦文舍利宝塔，又称开福寺舍利塔，因今景县原为景州所在地，所以人们通常称之为景州塔。该塔共十三层，外形为八面棱锥体，通高 63.85 米，底层周长 50.5 米，为砖石结构的密檐阁楼样式。景州塔于 1996 年被国务院列为第四批全国重点文物保护单位。

5. 河北赞皇治平寺石塔

治平寺石塔，又名嘉应寺石塔，坐落在河北省赞皇县嘉应寺村北的济水之滨。治平寺石塔高约 12.5 米，为八角仿木楼阁式，塔身分三层，各层均出檐，翼角微微翘起，整个塔纤细轻盈、挺拔庄重。

治平寺石塔于 1996 年被国务院列为第四批全国重点文物保护单位，这与其"年代古老"又是"仿木构"有关系。

木构建筑是中国古代建筑的主流，由于木材易损，所以隋唐时期的木构建筑留存稀少。而治平寺石塔上的仿木结构楼阁正是当时木构建筑形式的直接反映，斗拱、屋檐，是我们了解、还原唐代木结构建筑比例、结构做法和形式特征的重要实物依据。

此外，治平寺石塔石料切磨精致，雕饰精美丰富，堪称中国石雕佛塔中的瑰宝。塔上佛像故事石刻有 32 幅，佛、菩萨、力士等大小浮雕造像近百尊。佛像的袈裟、菩萨的长裙，雕琢出自然柔软的下垂曲线，力士的肌肉浑圆有力、线条清晰。

以上只是河北省古塔资源中的冰山一角，对这吉光片羽的一瞥，使我们在欣赏古塔建筑之美的同时，得以窥见燕赵大地深厚的历史文化底蕴。

赞皇治平寺石塔

第6章
河北大地上的国宝文物

历史并不是静止的，时光的漫漫长河中，流动着一代代先人奔腾不息的生命热血与创造活力。

文物也不是冰冷的，沧桑的件件物品上，凝结着一个个独特生命的辛劳智慧与情感温度。

文物，根据等级可分为珍贵文物和一般文物。珍贵文物，又分为一级、二级、三级文物。而一级文物过去还分为甲、乙两等。我们所说的"国宝"，通常指"一级甲等"文物。

河北拥有18件国宝级文物，它们分别出土于7处古遗址、古墓葬。细目如下：

出土地址及数量	文物名称
战国中山国遗址　7件	中山王厝铁足铜鼎、错金银四龙四凤铜方案座 错金银铜虎噬鹿屏座、十五连盏铜灯 银首人俑铜灯、中山王厝夔龙饰铜方壶 错金银铜版兆域图
西汉满城汉墓　5件	错金铜博山炉、长信宫灯、刘胜金缕玉衣 窦绾金缕玉衣、透雕双龙白玉璧
东汉中山穆王刘畅墓　2件	透雕神仙故事玉座屏、龙螭衔环谷纹青玉璧
战国燕下都遗址　1件	透雕龙凤纹铜铺首
元代窖藏遗址　1件	青花釉里红开光贴花盖罐
静志寺塔基地宫　1件	白釉刻花龙首净瓶
万堤古墓群　1件	何弘敬墓志铭

1. 中山王厝铁足铜鼎（战国中山国遗址）

中山王厝铁足铜鼎，1977年出土于河北平山县战国中山国王陵一号墓西库。鼎通高51.5厘米，口径42厘米，腹径65.8厘米，重60千克，铜身铁足，是目前考古发现的最

大的战国时期铜铁合铸器，而且鼎外壁刻有77行铭文，共计469字，是目前发现的铭文最长的战国青铜器。

铁足铜鼎铭文记述了中山国和战国时期的重要历史，弥补了史书中对中山王世系缺失记载的遗憾，还印证了史书中对一些重要历史事件的记载，具有极其重要的历史研究价值，因此于2002年列入首批禁止出境文物名录。现馆藏于河北省博物院。

中山王厝铁足铜鼎

2. 错金银四龙四凤铜方案座（战国中山国遗址）

错金银四龙四凤铜方案座的底座为圆环形，由4只（两雌两雄）跪卧的梅花鹿承托。鹿的四肢蜷曲，神态温顺，鹿身饰有错金斑纹，鹿的双颊饰有云头纹。底座的外壁饰勾连云纹，纹饰疏朗雅致，柔中带刚。底座向上呈凹弧面形，周边饰有卷云纹。在底座的弧面上，站立4条独首双尾的神龙，分向四方。龙挺胸昂首，前肢撑立，爪抓底座，肩有双翼，龙身向左右两侧蟠环相交，双翼反钩双角。龙的长颈及胸部饰鳞纹，中间蟠环处及双羽饰长羽纹，后尾部渐细饰蟒皮纹。相邻两龙蟠环交结处，均有长钩状彩羽形饰与中间壁形成拱状连接。龙身各处的纹饰洒脱舒展，自然沉稳，生动地刻画出龙的轩昂气度与独特风神。龙身蟠环纠结之间四面各有一引颈长鸣之凤，头顶花冠，颈饰花斑羽纹，翅饰长羽纹，垂尾饰修长花羽纹，生动华丽，典雅迷人。四龙的上吻各托住一个一

斗二升式斗拱，斗拱承托方形梁框，斗拱和案框上均饰勾连云纹。该斗拱是我国最早的斗拱应用实例。整个案座结构复杂，龙飞凤舞，其瑰丽的错金银纹饰多变而不显繁缛、生动而不显零乱，内容与形式、整体结构与线条细节的搭配和谐统一，回旋盘曲，拥有不拘一格的多样性，是错金银工艺中的一件瑰宝。现馆藏于河北省博物院。

错金银四龙四凤铜方案座

3. 错金银铜虎噬鹿屏座（战国中山国遗址）

错金银铜虎噬鹿屏座，座长 51 厘米、高 21.9 厘米、重 26.6 千克。器座以虎为主体，虎双目圆睁，两耳直竖，正在吞食一只柔弱的小鹿。小鹿在虎口中拼命挣扎，短尾用力上翘，始终无法脱身。虎后肢用力蹬地，前躯下踞，整个身躯呈弧形，虎的右前爪因抓鹿而悬空，座身平衡借用鹿腿支撑。整个器形构思巧妙而自然。虎、鹿皮毛斑纹均用金银镶错而成，生动逼真。

虎的项部和臀部各立一个长方形銎（qióng）。

错金银铜虎噬鹿屏座

銎两侧同饰山羊头面，羊口即为銎口。沿两銎口直线相交，可成 84 度交角，接近直角，安上屏扇恰成曲尺形。整件器物表现出虎、鹿的动态和身躯结构，增加了器物的艺术效果。此器物构思巧妙，铸工精湛，在国内十分罕见。现馆藏于河北省博物院。

4. 十五连盏铜灯（战国中山国遗址）

十五连盏铜灯，战国灯具。1977 年平山县三汲村战国中山国王厝墓出土，高 82.9 厘米，是战国时期出土的最高灯具。整体造型犹如一棵大树，主干矗立在镂空夔龙纹底座上，由三只独首双身、口衔圆环的猛虎托起。四周伸出七节树枝，枝上托起 15 盏灯盘，高低有序，错落有致。每节树枝均可拆卸，榫口形状各自不同，便于安装，并可根据需要增减灯盏的数目。架枝上塑有游动的夔龙、鸣叫的小鸟和顽皮嬉戏的群猴。树下站立赤膊短裳的鲜虞族家奴二人，正向树上抛食戏猴。底座上刻有铭文两处 24 字。现馆藏于河北省博物院。

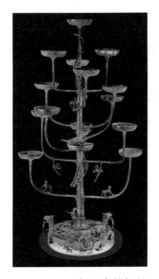

十五连盏铜灯

银首人俑铜灯

5. 银首人俑铜灯（战国中山国遗址）

此灯高 66.4 厘米，由铜质银首人、铜质蟠螭杆和铜质灯盘组成，以一男子作为该灯的结构主体部分，同时也是设计创意时重要的形象塑造中心。他立于兽纹方座正中，两臂侧平伸，青铜身躯上安放有银质人头，浓眉、短须、扁脸、高颧、嘴角微翘，眼睛以黑宝石镶嵌而成，炯炯有神；身着紧衣广袖，下裳曳地，分叉处露出双足，服饰上以卷云纹为饰，并添以黑、朱二色漆，更显其华丽非凡。人俑左手握住一螭尾，螭则横身翘首承托一灯盘，其又被盘卧于底盘中的另一蟠螭翘首攫噬；铜人右手也持蟠螭，此螭口衔错银龙纹灯柱，柱上绕以浮雕螭龙并有一攀缘之猴，呈游龙逐猴状，柱端顶一灯盘，为此灯的最高点。整体造型高低错落，外轮廓形成一个规整的直角三角形，人俑控制着蟠螭将分散的三个灯盘连贯起来真可谓匠心独运。三个灯盘皆为中空槽状环形，每盘三扦，有扦处灯盘底与侧壁均向外扩出，三盘九扦，数取"九"之极限应为有意安排。此灯不仅是目前所见装饰最为华丽、形式较复杂的战国灯具，也是高度较高的战国人俑灯具，是将实用性与装饰性有机结合的典范代表。现馆藏于河北省博物院。

中山王厝夔龙饰铜方壶

6. 中山王厝夔龙饰铜方壶（战国中山国遗址）

通高 63 厘米，最大径 35 厘米，重 28.72 公斤。礼器，造型独特，在它的四个光平的腹壁上，以纤细的笔触刻着优美的篆书，其铭文多达 450 字，铭文大意是中山王十四年，中山王命相邦司马赒，择所获燕国之吉金制成此壶。告诫嗣王记取燕国之反臣为主的教训，颂扬司马赒的忠信和伐燕的功绩，并阐明如何得贤、民附和巩固政权的道理。现馆藏于河北省博物院。

7. 错金银铜版兆域图（战国中山国遗址）

错金银铜版兆域图是用铜版制作的中山王陵区建设规划图，在铜版中嵌入金银薄片和银线，勾勒出王堂、王后堂、哀后堂和夫人堂等建筑规划，值得一提的是，规划图的指示方向和我们现在的通用方向是相反的，上南下北，左东右西。图里还有明确的五百分之一的比例尺和详细的文字说明，有 24 处用"尺"作为单位标记，有 14 处用"步"作为单位标记，是目前世界上发现的最早的有比例铜版建筑规划图。现馆藏于河北省博物院。

错金银铜版兆域图

8. 错金铜博山炉（西汉满城汉墓）

错金铜博山炉，1968 年出土于河北满城中山靖王刘胜墓，这是西汉时作为香薰炉用的青铜器，因为造型象征的是传说中的海上仙山——博山，所以叫做博山炉。

这件错金博山炉随葬的墓主中山靖王刘胜，是汉景帝刘启的庶子，他最为人熟知的就是生活骄奢淫逸，非"高奢品"不用，大名鼎鼎的国宝金缕玉衣和长信宫灯就是从他的墓中出土的，所以错金博山炉被称为"史上最豪华的香薰"也是有迹可循的，其整体极为精致和华美。现馆藏于河北博物院。

错金铜博山炉

长信宫灯

9. 长信宫灯（西汉满城汉墓）

长信宫灯，西汉的一件铜鎏金青铜器，大约制成于公元前 151 年，距今已经 2 200 多年了。这盏灯于 1968 年在中山靖王刘胜之妻窦绾墓出土，因为灯身上刻有"长信"的铭文，所以取名叫长信宫灯。现馆藏于河北博物院。

10. 刘胜金缕玉衣（西汉满城汉墓）

刘胜金缕玉衣 1968 年 5 月出土于保定满城中山靖王墓，现藏于河北博物院。

玉衣全长 1.88 米，共用玉片 2 498 片，金丝约 1 100 克。玉衣的外观和男子体型一样，宽肩阔胸，腹部突鼓，四肢粗壮，腹下有男性生殖器罩盒，头部有高高隆起的鼻子，三个狭窄的缝隙代表双眼和嘴。玉衣分为头部、上衣、袖筒、裤筒、手套和鞋六个部分，每一部分都可以彼此分离，犹如制衣工人裁剪缝制的一件衣服。其中头部由脸盖和头罩构成，上衣由前片、后片构成，袖筒、裤筒、手套和鞋都是左右分开的。所用玉片大部分呈长方形和方形，也有梯形、三角形、四边形和多边形。最大的玉片长 4.5 厘米，宽 3.5 厘米，用在脚底。最小的玉片只有成人拇指盖大小，用来表现手指。与金缕玉衣相伴的还有鎏金镶玉铜枕、玉九窍塞、玉握和 18 件殓尸用玉璧，组成一套规格最高的汉代丧葬用玉。

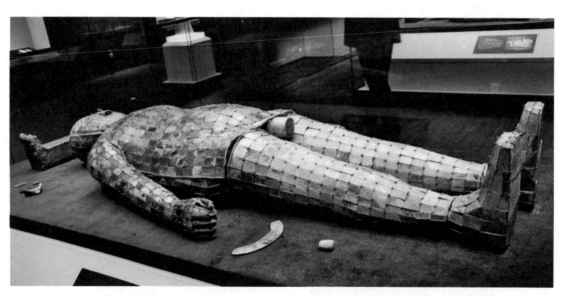

刘胜金缕玉衣

11. 窦绾金缕玉衣（西汉满城汉墓）

窦绾金缕玉衣，1968 年满城中山靖王刘胜妻窦绾墓出土。玉衣全长 1.72 米，玉片为岫岩玉，多数呈纯绿色，夹有灰白、黄褐色。玉衣分为五部分，共用玉片 2 160 片，金丝约 700 克组成。玉衣形式与刘胜墓的相似，头下有鎏金镶玉铜枕。现馆藏于河北博物院。

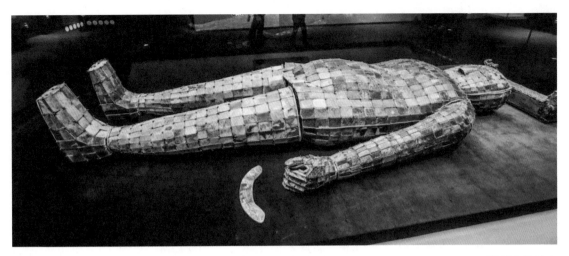

窦绾金缕玉衣

12. 透雕双龙白玉璧（西汉满城汉墓）

透雕双龙白玉璧 1968 年于满城陵山中山靖王刘胜墓出土。文物通体高 25.9 厘米、玉璧外径 13.4 厘米。

透雕双龙白玉璧玉质晶莹洁白，玉璧两面雕琢着细密谷纹，周边起棱。玉璧上端有透雕双龙卷云纹高纽，纹样优美，造型生动，雕琢精致，为汉代玉器中的珍品。现馆藏于河北博物院。

透雕双龙白玉璧

13. 透雕神仙故事玉座屏（东汉中山穆王刘畅墓）

透雕神仙故事玉座屏出土于东汉中山穆王刘畅墓。定州为汉代中山国国都，历时 300 余年，东西两汉共有 17 代中山王，这位叫做刘畅的是第十六代，也就是东汉第六代中山王。

透雕神仙故事玉座屏由四块透雕玉片插接而成。两侧以双胜为支架，双胜主体纹饰为透雕青龙、白虎纹；中间两屏片略呈半月形，两端有榫插入架内，透雕人物鸟兽纹饰。上屏片正中为"西王母"，分发高髻，凭几端坐，旁有朱雀、狐狸、三足乌等；下屏片正中为"东王公"，发后梳，凭几而坐，旁有侍者及熊、玄武等。其纹饰形象地反映了汉代人的神仙崇拜思想。现馆藏于定州博物馆。

透雕神仙故事玉座屏

龙螭衔环谷纹青玉璧

透雕龙凤纹铜铺首

青花釉里红开光贴花盖罐

14. 龙螭衔环谷纹青玉璧（东汉中山穆王刘畅墓）

龙螭衔环谷纹青玉璧出土于东汉中山穆王刘畅墓。现藏于定州博物馆。

此璧通高 30.5 厘米，用新疆和田青玉雕制，玉质半透明，表面有温润、明亮的光泽，局部沁蚀处泛红褐色。璧之内、外边缘为素面宽带；上部透雕龙螭衔环钮，两侧分别透雕一龙一螭，龙螭口、鼻、眼、耳及足均以阴线勾勒；璧面雕饰整齐的谷纹。玉璧是古人祭祀用的礼器，"以苍璧礼天"，认为其中的圆形孔可以通天，使人特别是统治者与天得以沟通。谷为我国先民最早栽培成功的粮食作物之一，到了汉代，谷物的种植成为最重要的农事活动。民以食为天，汉统治者把农业作为国之根本，古代祭天首先要祭祀农神，把谷纹用于礼器上的装饰内容，显示统治者是为了以此寻求五谷丰登、国泰民安。通过玉璧以礼的形式把神权和王权相结合，反映了当时天人感应的意识，也体现了统治者通过"敬天、保民、明德"，以求江山永存。

15. 透雕龙凤纹铜铺首（战国燕下都遗址）

透雕龙凤纹铜铺首，1966 年出土于保定市易县的燕下都遗址老姆台，高 74.5 厘米，宽 36.8 厘米，重 21.5 千克。现收藏于河北博物院，是河北博物院的十大镇馆之宝之一，也是中国第一大青铜宫门铺首。

铺首是含有驱邪意义的传统建筑大门上的装饰物，在古代社会人们认为要阻挡妖魔鬼怪进门，最主要的方法是在大门上放一怪兽衔着门环，可以防止妖魔鬼怪进门，铺首，是最原始的"门拉手"，可以用来开门、敲门，同时也具有装饰意义。据专家推测，这件透雕龙凤纹铜铺首可能是燕下都宫殿大门上的构件。

16. 青花釉里红开光贴花盖罐（元代窖藏遗址）

青花釉里红开光贴花盖罐出土于河北省保定市，通高 41 厘米，口径 15.5 厘米，足径 18.5 厘米，现馆藏于河北博物院。

青花釉里红开光贴花盖罐的盖子顶部有一个坐着的狮形雕塑，用来打开罐子的把手。罐盖上描绘着青花莲瓣纹、卷草纹以及回纹，美观华丽，极具魅力。罐壁从上往下，由薄变厚，整个罐子丰满浑厚，纹饰层次鲜明，青花、釉里红在作品中相互衬托，红色、蓝色交相辉映，整体气度雍容华贵。

17. 白釉刻花龙首净瓶（北宋净众院塔基地宫出土）

白釉刻花龙首净瓶，1969 年出土于定州市净众院塔基地宫，现藏于定州市博物馆。

此瓶高 60.9 厘米，腹径 19.1 厘米，底径 10.1 厘米。瓶细长颈，颈中部出沿，颈上部为仰覆莲瓣纹，中部为覆莲纹相轮圆盘，下部为竹节纹。圆肩、鼓腹、卧足。肩部饰三重覆莲纹，一侧塑有龙首短流，龙首高昂，怒目，张口露齿，下颌饰一缕龙须。上腹刻缠枝花卉，下腹刻仰莲四重，刀法犀利，线条流畅，具有浅浮雕效果。定窑产品以小型器物为主，大器十分少见。此件器物形体高大，造型隽秀，装饰华丽，为定窑瓷器中最为精美的一件。

白釉刻花龙首净瓶

何弘敬墓志铭

18. 何弘敬墓志铭

墓志边长 1.95 米，厚 0.53 米，是我国已出土唐代墓志铭中尺寸最大的一方。墓志雕工精美、神态生动，图案简练，线条流畅。墓志上描述墓主人生平事迹的碑文用楷书镌写，共 60 行，满行 58 字，共 3 800 字。现馆藏于邯郸市大名县石刻博物馆。

第2篇
荣光岁月　红色之美

　　河北有着光荣的革命传统和革命历史，是中国共产党主要创始人之一李大钊的故乡，是中共党组织建立最早的省份之一。大革命时期，河北原野风雷激荡，革命斗争波澜壮阔。抗日战争时期，河北成为敌后抗日的主战场，中国第一个敌后抗日根据地——晋察冀抗日根据地就诞生在太行山东侧的燕赵大地；晋察冀边区政府、八路军129师司令部坐落在这里；为了粉碎日本帝国主义的扫荡，河北抗日军民创造性地利用地道战、地雷战和平原游击战打击日寇，留下了诸如冉庄地道遗址等重要红色遗迹。解放战争时期，河北既是中国革命领导中心，又是解放战争的主要战场之一。西柏坡是中国最后一个农村指挥所，中国从这里开始新的篇章。红色记忆，是河北不可磨灭的光荣历史，感受红色氛围，是河北大地最具特色的人文景观。

第 7 章

西柏坡

—— 新中国从这里走来

　　滹沱河在燕赵大地上一路奔腾，至河北省石家庄平山县时拐了个弯，环抱起一座静谧的村庄，这就是西柏坡。

　　西柏坡，这个冀西山区滹沱河北岸的小山村，风光秀丽，水土肥美。它是解放战争时期中央工作委员会（以下简称中央工委）、中共中央和解放军总部的所在地，党中央和毛主席在此指挥了决定解放战争走向的辽沈、淮海、平津三大战役，召开了具有伟大历史意义的七届二中全会和全国土地会议，之后全国解放，故有"新中国从这里走来""中国命运定于此村"的美誉。

西柏坡

1947年5月，刘少奇、朱德率中央工委进驻西柏坡。1948年5月，毛泽东、周恩来、任弼时率中共中央和解放军总部来到西柏坡与中央工委会合，西柏坡成为当时中国革命的领导中心。在这里，召开了中国共产党全国土地会议，通过了《中国土地法大纲》，实现了耕者有其田；指挥了辽沈、淮海、平津三大战役，取得了战略决战的决定性胜利，使这个普通的山村成为"解放全中国的最后一个农村指挥所"；召开了中共七届二中全会，描绘了新中国宏伟的蓝图。1949年3月23日，中共中央和解放军总部离开西柏坡赴京建国。

中共中央离开后，建屏县（1958年改为平山县）政府对中央机关留下的物品进行了交接。为了保护革命遗址和文物，1955年成立了西柏坡纪念馆筹备处。1982年3月11日，国务院公布西柏坡中共中央旧址为全国重点文物保护单位。

1992年以来，相继修建了西柏坡石刻园、西柏坡国家安全教育馆、西柏坡廉政教育馆、领袖风范雕塑园、五大书记铜铸像、西柏坡纪念碑、周恩来评语碑、西柏坡文物保护碑、西柏坡青少年绿色文明园等革命传统教育系列工程，极大地丰富了爱国主义教育的内容。目前，西柏坡爱国主义教育基地已经形成了一个完整的、多层次的革命传统教育体系。

西柏坡中共中央旧址占地1 644平方米，被一道土灰白墙围定，院内有毛泽东、朱德、刘少奇、周恩来、任弼时、董必武同志的旧居，中央军委作战室、九月会议旧址、中共七届二中全会旧址等17处。简陋的小平房里陈列着当年领袖们工作、生活用过的用具。油漆斑驳的办公桌、老式的电话机、马灯、陈旧的椅子、沙发，还有那密密麻麻的军事地图……再现了老一辈革命家在西柏坡的艰苦岁月，讴歌了伟人们为新中国成立而建树的丰功伟绩。

西柏坡陈列展览馆于 1976 年 10 月开工。1978 年 5 月 26 日，为纪念中共中央和解放军总部移驻西柏坡 30 周年，与中共中央旧址同时开放。陈列展览馆里内设的基本陈列曾于 1993 年、1996 年、1998 年和 2003 年相继进行了修改完善和大规模的改陈更新，曾被国家文物局评为"全国十大精品陈列"。目前的基本陈列"新中国从这里走来"获得"全国十大精品陈列特别奖"的殊荣。整个陈列共分 12 个展室（含序厅），以平山人民光辉的抗日斗争为铺垫，以解放战争为主线，展现中央工委和中共中央在西柏坡的伟大革命实践，重点介绍全国土地会议、三大战役、七届二中全会等重大历史事件，利用声、光、电等高科技陈展手段和现代陈展理念，生动鲜明地突出"新中国从西柏坡走来"的展览主题。

　　如今，西柏坡已成为全国著名的红色旅游胜地，参观人数逐年上升。一批批参观者怀着崇敬的心情，从四面八方来到西柏坡追忆老一辈革命家在这里的峥嵘岁月，寻觅西柏坡精神的真谛。

第 8 章
冉庄地道
——易守难攻的地下长城

　　河北省保定市清苑冉庄地道战遗址，是抗战时期中华民族以弱胜强伟大创举的典范，也是全世界人民反抗法西斯侵略的二战奇迹。岁月流逝，昔日硝烟弥漫的抗日战场，如今早已是祥和宁静的美丽家园。可是，沉于地下的那座"钢铁长城"，却用不争的事实，在后人心中激起向前的力量。1965 年，红色电影《地道战》一经公映，不仅成为传世经典，更使冉庄名扬天下。

　　行走在冉庄地道战遗址保护区内，耳边回响着《毛主席的话儿记心上》那动人的旋律，一切都那么平静安然。但地面隐藏的射击口、民房高墙上的各种工事，以及地下蜿蜒的长城，都在默默无言地诉说着那段沧桑岁月。

冉庄地道战纪念馆

冉庄村里的十字街，维持了 20 世纪三四十年代的模样。村口那棵虽已枯朽却依然挺拔的老槐树，正是五十多年前《地道战》中的老槐树，电影中村支书高老忠快步跑向老槐树敲钟报警的情节，就是在这里拍摄的。这棵老槐树已有千年的历史，在冀中平原上，这样的古树是罕见的。据说当年老槐树枝繁叶茂，上面也的确悬挂了古钟，专门用于报警之用。如今作为历史的见证和珍贵的文物，老槐树已被用钢筋混凝土加固，成为永久的革命传统教育场所。

凝聚无穷智慧的冉庄地道，有几个最明显的特点：三通，即高房互通、院落互通、地道互通；三交叉，即暗枪眼和明枪眼交叉，地堡和高房工事交叉，地堡火力和墙壁火力交叉；四好，即好藏、好钻、好打、好转移；五防，即防封锁、防破坏、防火烧、防水灌、防毒气。地道里面建有指挥部、储粮处、休息室、小型兵工厂等设施，指挥部就在十字街下。冉庄人民以冉庄十字街为中心，顺沿东、西、南、北大街挖掘了 4 条主干线，另有 24 条支线，形成了长达 32 里的地道网，地道的隐蔽射击孔遍布全村。

当时整个冀中平原村村有地道，地道长达 25 000 里，是一座名副其实的地下长城，更是一个顽强不屈的民族在残酷的战争环境中，在无险可守的大平原上创造的中国乃至世界战争史上的奇迹。

冉庄地道战遗址已于 1961 年被国务院列为全国首批重点文物保护单位。同时，它还是全国爱国主义教育示范基地、全国青少年教育基地、全国首批国防教育示范基地、全国百家红色旅游经典景区之一，2014 年入选国务院确定的第一批国家级抗战纪念设施、遗址名录。

2010 年 9 月，冉庄地道战纪念馆新馆正式面向游客开放。新馆总建筑面积近 4 000 平方米，布展面积 1 800 平方米。馆内珍藏着大量珍贵的革命文物，其中国家一级革命文物 4 件、二级革命文物 17 件、三级革命文物 77 件。在纪念馆展厅入口处，一面从 1931 年到 1945 年的浮雕墙，仿若时光隧道，将人们带回那战火纷飞的年代。新馆布展以"抗战奇观，地下长城"为主题，从冀中沦陷、国民蒙难，到力挽狂澜，地道战大显神威，名扬天下。纪念馆采用现代设计语言与写实造景相结合的手法，同时充实了大量的革命文物、照片、图表、雕塑、绘画创作，利用丰富的陈展手法和高新技术让展览更具参与性。

据统计，经受了血与火考验的冉庄人民在中国共产党的领导下，不畏强暴，奋起抗争，利用地道优势在抗日战争和解放战争中对敌作战 157 次，歼敌 2 100 多人，冉庄也因此荣获"地道战模范村"的光荣称号，2007 年被确定为全国历史文化名村。1950 年，36 个国家的代表团来参观，对神奇的冉庄地道战赞叹不已。现在，冉庄保留着 30 万平方米的遗址保护区，来参观的游客每年都达到 100 万人次以上。冉庄地道战遗址是融爱国主义教育、国防教育和旅游于一体、独具特色的理想参观地，也为后人留下了一处永恒的宝贵的历史财富。

第9章
晋察冀边区革命纪念馆
——新中国的雏形在这里诞生

　　晋察冀边区革命纪念馆位于保定市阜平县城南庄镇，它的前身是"城南庄革命纪念馆"，其中晋察冀军区司令部旧址 1994 年被列为省级爱国主义教育基地，1996 年被定为国家级重点文物保护单位，2005 年被列为全国爱国主义教育示范基地。

　　1937 年聂荣臻同志以阜平为起点创建了晋察冀抗日根据地，是我党我军创建的第一块敌后抗日根据地。它不仅是华北抗战的坚强堡垒，也是对日进行战略反攻和解放战争时期我军进军东北、夺取华北的前沿阵地。晋察冀边区创立的崭新的民主制度和完善的建构为新中国政权建设积累了十分宝贵的经验，它是全国抗日的模范、执行方针的模范、统一战线的模范、根据地建设的模范、人民战争的模范，因此，晋察冀边区被称为"新民主主义社会的雏形""新中国的雏形"，被毛泽东同志亲笔授予"模范抗日根据地"的光荣称号。1948 年 4 月毛主席率领中央机关从陕北来到晋察冀边区阜平县城南庄，居住工作了很长一段时间，期间，召开中共中央书记处扩大会议，审时度势，调整了南线战略，为三大战役的胜利奠定了坚实的基础。毛主席还亲自起草了《纪念一九四八年五一劳动节口号》，第一次具体描绘了新中国的蓝图，成为新中国成立的动员令。

　　整个景区由展览馆、雕塑广场、晋察冀军区司令部旧址和后山防空洞等组成，总占地面积为 14.7 万平方米。展览馆展厅面积 1 700 平方米，展线长度 260 米，展出文物 259 件、照片 222 张、图表 31 块。展览内容共分为六部分，按照历史的发展脉络从根据地的创立到中共中央移驻晋察冀进行安排。第一部分是"建立第一个敌后抗日根据地"，重点介绍抗战爆发后，八路军出师华北，取得"平型关战役"胜利后奉党中央命令建立了敌后第一个根据地。第二部分是"坚持敌后游击战争"，重点介绍面对日军的进攻，八路军及边区人民运用多种形式抗击日军及在抗日战争中涌现的抗日烈士和英雄模范。第三部分是边区在党建、政权建设、经济建设、教育建设、文化建设等方面所取得的成绩。第四部分是"夺取抗战胜利"，重点介绍从 1944 年开始，晋察冀军区部队进行大练兵，发动系列战役，为对日反攻做好准备。第五部分是"踏上解放战争新征程"，重点介绍由于国民党坚持内战，晋察冀野战军寻找战机，取得了清风店战役和石家庄战役的胜利。

第六部分是"中共中央移驻晋察冀"，重点介绍 1948 年毛主席率党中央来到晋察冀解放区，进行土地改革，召开书记处扩大会议，组建华北区党政军机构，为三大战役的胜利奠定了基础。展览内容充分体现了"模范抗日根据地"的主题，并运用大量珍贵的照片、文物以及使用先进的声、光、电等手段，采取景观复原、幻影成像、触摸屏、雕塑等多种形式，对展览内容进行详细、生动地说明，展示了晋察冀边区军民可歌可泣的英雄事迹和为中华民族解放事业建立的不朽功勋。

雕塑广场矗立有聂荣臻和美穗子、红色新闻战士、李勇和爆破组、戎冠秀与受伤战士、国际友人白求恩、狼牙山五壮士六组青铜雕塑，这些雕塑作品从不同侧面反映了晋察冀根据地可歌可泣的斗争历史。

旧址区有两重院落，是 1947 年秋聂荣臻司令员率领军区机关从张家口撤离回到阜平修建的。前院矗立着晋察冀军区司令员聂荣臻的铜像，气势恢宏。院中栽有桧柏、银杏和榕树，鸟儿在树枝间啾鸣，不失清静和幽雅。后院是晋察冀军区司令部旧址，包括三排土坯房。1948 年毛泽东、周恩来率领中央机关从延安来到这里，其中有毛主席、周恩来、

晋察冀边区革命纪念馆

任弼时等中央领导同志的住宿和办公室，还有军区作战科、电话室和会议室。这是晋察冀军区司令部在河北唯一完整保留的机关旧址以及毛主席进京之前唯一完整保留的居住旧址，原址原貌，原汁原味。后山脚下还有一条长约 128 米的防空洞，是由晋察冀军区工兵连的战士人工挖凿而成的，依旧保存完好。

纪念馆环境优美，北靠菩萨岭，南临胭脂河。当年，陈毅同志曾在这里为聂荣臻同志写下了"十年驻马胭脂河"的壮丽诗句。馆内周围松柏苍翠，绿草如茵，繁花似锦；馆外青山耸立，林木葱茏，造就了庄重肃穆又富有自然情趣的观览和休憩环境。

第10章
河北石家庄小灰楼
—— 见证新中国金融事业起步

　　河北省石家庄市繁华的中华北大街 55 号，坐落着一幢三层水泥砖混结构小楼。因其表面呈青灰色，当地人亲切地称之为"小灰楼"。中国人民银行在这里成立，第一套人民币也诞生于此。

　　"小灰楼"始建于 1940 年，最早是日伪华北建设总署和石门河渠工程处办公室。日本投降后，国民党先遣部队抢占石家庄，将此作为司令部。1947 年 11 月 12 日，石家庄解放后成为中共石家庄市委办公地点，后移交给冀南银行和晋察冀边区银行使用。1948 年 12 月 1 日，中国人民银行在这里正式挂牌办公，同时人民币正式发行，石家庄成为第一个使用人民币的城市。

　　在中国共产党领导中华民族历经艰难困苦走向胜利的过程中，金融工作一直伴随着红色政权的发展而发展。从土地革命到抗日战争一直到中华人民共和国诞生前夕，人民政权被分割成彼此不能连接的区域。各根据地建立了相对独立、分散管理的根据地银行，并各自发行在本根据地内流通的货币。这些革命早期的金融工作，在中国革命胜利的进程中发挥了独特而重要的作用。这种金融状态，直到 1947 年解放战争即将由战略防御转为战略进攻时，才开始有了实质性转变。

　　为克服财经困难，保障战争供给，"动员一切力量，全力准备反攻"，1947 年 3 月 25 日，经中共中央批准，在晋冀鲁豫解放区的武安县冶陶镇召开华北财经会议，商讨统一财经问题。参会代表涉及各大解放区，为了统一思想，中央派董必武由陕北前往指导会议。董必武带着夫人、孩子和工作人员一路东行，在途经山西省五台县时，所带的干粮吃完了。董必武拿出陕甘宁边区银行所发行的货币交给随行的同志，让他到旁边的小店里买点吃的。结果，当地老百姓不认这个票子，说什么都不肯收下。最后，他们不得已用新布料换取了食物。经过此事，董必武切身感受到统一货币的必要性和迫切性。

　　1947 年 4 月，华北财经会议期间，中央决定成立华北财经办事处，着手统一华北各解放区财经政策，调节各解放区财经关系，董必武被任命为主任。1947 年 10 月 2 日，董必武致电中共中央，建议"组建中央银行，发行统一货币"，并建议银行名称为"中国人民银行"，得到中共中央电复肯定。随后，华北财经办事处在平山县夹峪村成立了中国人民银行筹备处，由曾经担任过陕甘宁边区财政厅厅长、时任华北财经办事处副主任的南汉宸担任筹备处主任。随着华北重镇石家庄解放，经上级批准，冀南银行与晋察冀边区银行于 1948 年 4 月 12 日迁至石家庄市原中华北街 11 号（现中华北大街 55 号）的"小灰楼"内合署办公。同时，中国人民银行筹备处也从平山县夹峪村搬到了"小灰楼"。

搞经济的同志们干劲冲天，紧锣密鼓地建银行、印钞票，为发行统一货币做准备。早在 1947 年 11 月前，晋察冀边区银行印刷局就已经完成几种版别的票样设计稿。当绘有毛泽东头像的第一套人民币设计票版报请中共中央审查时，被毛泽东婉言谢绝。他说："票子是政府发行的，不是党发行的，现在我是党的主席，而不是政府的主席，因此，票子上不能印我的像。"于是，董必武又组织人员重新设计，提出将人民币主图主景改为"反映解放区工农业生产建设图景"的建议。最终，由晋察冀边区印刷局经验丰富的设计师王益久、沈乃镛设计完成了第一套人民币的样稿。

1948 年 12 月 1 日，华北人民政府"金字第四号"布告宣告成立中国人民银行，发行新币。当日，中国人民银行在"小灰楼"宣告成立。首批人民币印出后，立即被送往西柏坡，由董必武面呈毛泽东审阅。毛泽东望着崭新的人民币，高兴地说："人民有了自己的武装，有了自己的政权，有了自己的土地，现在又有了自己的银行和货币，这才真正是人民当家作主啊！"当天，在石家庄和平山县同时发行了面额 10 元、50 元的人民银行新币，人民币正式诞生。第一套人民币共计 12 种面额、62 种版别，由董必武题写了"中国人民银行" 6 个字，到 1955 年 3 月停止流通。中国人民银行成立和第一套人民币发行，在中国金融史、货币史上都具有划时代的重大意义。它标志着在中国共产党领导的新民主主义革命胜利前夕，革命根据地解放区的金融机构及其货币由分散到统一的过程，结束了国民党统治下几十年的币制混乱历史。

1949 年 1 月，北平和平解放，从 2 月起，中国人民银行开始陆续由"小灰楼"迁往北平。而人民银行总行直属印刷厂（即印钞厂）则从石家庄西北的柏林庄迁到"小灰楼"里，继续印制第一套人民币。当时印钞厂在"小灰楼"对外挂的是"民众书店"的牌子，直到 1950 年初，印钞厂与北京人民印刷厂合并，才搬出了"小灰楼"。"小灰楼"的历史使命暂告一段落。

2009 年 12 月 1 日，修复竣工后的"小灰楼"以中国人民银行旧址纪念馆暨河北钱币博物馆的新形象重新对外开放，并被列入全国重点文物保护单位、"中国 20 世纪建筑遗产项目"名录，重新焕发出熠熠光彩。它见证了新中国金融事业的起步，记录着那段红色历史。

第11章

平山团

——太行山上铁的子弟兵

    河北省平山县位于太行山东麓、滹沱河上游，是石家庄西部的一个山区县，革命圣地西柏坡就坐落在平山县的中部。说到平山县西柏坡，人们都知道"新中国从这里走来"，这个原本极为平凡的小山村已经载入史册，成为平山人乃至河北人的骄傲。平山县还有一个值得骄傲、值得载入史册的团体，这就是平山团。

    20世纪30年代初，平山县便燃起了革命的火种。1934年底，平山县第一个加入中国共产党的党员栗再温重返家乡，参与平山县委的领导工作，从此，革命的洪流在平山县汹涌澎湃、不可阻挡。1937年9月，在抗日前线取得平型关大捷的八路军乘胜东进，开辟敌后抗日根据地。9月28日，八路军120师359旅副旅长王震率部来到平山县洪子店，向平山县委的同志传达了党中央关于创建抗日根据地、开展敌后游击战的指示精神，号召平山县的共产党员组织平山人民抗日救国，用生命和热血保卫家乡。时任冀西特委书记栗再温、平山县委书记王昭带领平山县的共产党员，迅速组成了10个扩军小组，分赴各个村镇宣传动员。一时间，平山县沸腾了，"抗日救国，人人有责""参加八路军，赶走小东洋"等抗战口号响彻太行，抗战的标语刷满街巷，抗战的歌声激越嘹亮……

    参加八路军意味着什么？意味着随时可能为国捐躯，因此，富于牺牲精神的平山共产党员带头参军。平山县委委员梁雨晴动员家乡的党员集体入伍，仅有60多户人家的猫石村一下子走出了34名八路军战士，梁雨晴担任八路军平山团第一营第一连第一排排长。平山县第一位农民党员、第一位农村党支部书记李法庄，率领霍宾台村60多名青壮年赶赴洪子店集体参军。父子相随入伍、兄弟结伴参军、师生一同从戎的感人场面，出现在平山的山村、乡镇。短短1个月零3天，从12岁到50多岁的平山子弟，陆陆续续加入抗日队伍，组成了兵员1 700人的平山团。11月7日，在一片激动人心的锣鼓声中，平山团离开洪子店，跟随120师359旅开赴抗日前线。1938年1月，罗荣桓率领115师教导队来到洪子店，希望栗再温帮助扩充兵员，参军的热潮再度涌动，平山县又有1 700名子弟跟随115师挺进鲁东南，成为115师的平山团。据统计，抗战期间，仅有25万人口的平山县陆续输送12 065名英雄儿女参加八路军。

开赴抗日前线的平山团英勇善战，立下了赫赫战功。1938 年 3 月 11 日，718 团 2 营与 717 团在岢岚县三井镇围歼日军第 26 师团千田大队，毙伤日军 300 余人，俘虏日军 28 人；6 月 10 日，718 团 2 营、3 营在浑源县南晋家庄战斗中，将日军 300 多人困在一条狭长地带，集中火力猛烈打击，毙伤日军 100 余人；9 月 24 日至 30 日，718 团团长陈宗尧率 1 营、3 营阻击进攻灵丘的日军，占领有利地形，利用夜战灵活性，步步紧逼，竟然逼得日军 100 人跳崖……

1938 年 11 月，718 团参谋长左齐在伏击日军运输大队的战斗中左臂受伤，白求恩大夫连夜为他做右肩关节离断手术，保住了他的生命。当白求恩得知这些小伙子都来自平山时感到十分惊讶，高兴地与他们攀谈，告诉战士们他刚刚从平山来，并用生硬的汉语发音说出"平山"两个字，战士们都笑了。白求恩对清一色平山子弟组成的平山团感情很深，在日记和信件中亲切地称他们是"朴实可爱的孩子""穿着军装的劳动人民""他们平均年龄是 22 岁……通常是些大个子，六英尺高，强壮而黝黑，一举一动又沉着，又有明确的目的性，有一种果敢的风度。为他们服务，确实是一种幸福……"经过白求恩大夫的精心治疗，平山团 71 名伤员重返抗日前线。

1939 年 5 月，717 团在日军"扫荡"中被包抄，718 团紧急驰援。在战斗中对日军形成反包围，展开近距离肉搏战。这次战斗激战 7 天 7 夜，共毙伤日军 1 000 余人，其中击毙敌人 600 多人，俘虏敌人 11 人，仅 3 营战士王家川一人就杀死了 8 个日寇。此外，还缴获九二式步兵炮 2 门、迫击炮 3 门，轻重机枪 22 挺、步马枪 800 多支，战马 200 多匹。这一战打出了平山团的威风和英名。捷报传来，晋察冀军区司令聂荣臻于 5 月 20 日通令嘉奖平山团，授予平山团"太行山上铁的子弟兵"光荣称号，指出："平山团的全体指战员们，特别发扬了我八路军的光荣传统，不顾一切牺牲，最坚决地把深入的敌人歼灭在山地里，这是平山团全体指战员同志最光荣的胜利纪录……你们是平山子弟的优秀武装，边区子弟的优秀武装，你们是太行山上铁的子弟兵！"这是"子弟兵"一词首次用于称呼共产党领导下的人民武装。5 月 28 日，《抗敌报》全文转发聂荣臻司令的嘉奖令，"平山团""子弟兵"这两个词语不胫而走，传遍华北大地。

为什么"子弟兵"这个称呼很快就能家喻户晓？因为它深受人民群众和人民军队指战员的喜爱，因为它饱含着人民军队和老百姓之间同呼吸、共命运的鱼水深情，因为它深刻地诠释了中国共产党领导下的人民武装来源于人民、根植于人民的新型军民关系。著名民主人士李公朴先生 1940 年春到晋察冀考察后，撰写了《华北敌后——晋察冀》一书，他在书中称颂道："子弟兵是老百姓的儿子，是在晋察冀生了根的抗日军。"此后，"人民子弟兵"作为抗日军民对共产党领导下的人民武装的亲切称谓，传遍全国，并沿用至今。

第 12 章

喜峰口长城抗战

——一把大刀砍出民族血性

地处唐山市迁西县北部的喜峰口，是万里长城众多关隘中的一个。1933 年，一场抵御外侮的战斗在这里爆发——500 壮士手持大刀砍向敌人，打击了日本侵略者的嚣张气焰，砍出了中国人的凛凛威风！喜峰口战役，成为中国抗战史上浓墨重彩的一笔。

喜峰口长城抗战遗址占地面积 2 800 亩，以 1933 年喜峰口长城抗战大捷这一历史事件为主题，以著名爱国歌曲《大刀进行曲》诞生地、著名抗日名句"宁为战死鬼，不做

喜峰雄关大刀园雕塑

亡国奴"发生的地点地等特色鲜明的爱国主义文化为主轴，先后修建了喜峰口长城抗战纪念碑、长城抗战诗句纪念墙、"大刀向鬼子头上砍去"主题雕塑、"铭记历史、强我中华"大刀礼赞、抗战烈士公墓、喜峰口长城抗战博物馆、喜峰口长城抗战纪念展厅、冀东抗战魂展厅等历史人文景观。

"九一八"事变后，东三省沦陷。1933 年 3 月，日本侵略军进逼长城，欲从喜峰口破关而入，平津危急。宋哲元、赵登禹等爱国将领率国民革命军第 29 军火速赶赴喜峰口长城一带抵御，同日军展开殊死搏斗。

在博物馆的玻璃橱窗里，当年砍杀过敌人的大刀依旧寒光凛凛，锋刃毕现。面对装备精良的日本侵略军，29 军选出 500 精兵强将组成大刀敢死队，决心以血肉之躯与敌人短兵相接，誓死保卫国土。为鼓舞士气，军长宋哲元写下"宁为战死鬼，不做亡国奴"的手令，通告全军。

1933 年 3 月 11 日深夜，喜峰口前线总指挥 29 军 109 旅旅长赵登禹、副旅长何基沣率领大刀队队员，夜袭敌营。此时，一众日军睡意正酣。大刀队队员们如同神兵天降，扑向敌营，抢起大刀，横杀竖砍，刀起头落……大刀队在敌营英勇拼杀了近 3 个小时，500 多名日本鬼子号叫着人头搬家。

据史料记载，以夜袭敌营为代表的喜峰口战役，是自"九一八"之后中国军队抗击日本侵略者的首次胜利，被列为中外军事史上"以少胜多、以弱胜强"的经典战例之一。据统计，喜峰口长城抗战累计消灭日军 5 300 余人，而中国军队亦为此付出巨大牺牲：500 大刀敢死队员为国捐躯 477 人，仅生还 23 人。

喜峰口长城抗战遗址现在已经建设成为喜峰雄关大刀园，成为全国红色旅游经典景区、河北省爱国主义教育基地、河北省国防教育基地。喜峰口长城抗战遗址也被列入第二批国家级抗战纪念设施、遗址名录。

第 3 篇
百年征程　谱写新时代篇章

奋斗是河北人民的优良品格和精神特质。传承和弘扬伟大奋斗精神，河北人民在革命、建设、改革发展中创造了一个又一个非凡奇迹。

从一棵树到一片林海，塞罕坝造就的不仅是"美丽高岭"，更是"奋斗奇迹"，塞罕坝人接力传承，续写着新时代的绿色传奇，而那一抹绿色，也走进越来越多河北人的心里。

从一片一望无际的原野，到一笔一画勾勒发展蓝图，"千年秀林"郁郁葱葱，白洋淀碧波万顷，京雄城际铁路开通运营，未来之城拔节生长。不断赶超的"雄安高度"，折射河北勇往直前的奋进姿态。

塞外小城崇礼开启"冰雪奇缘"。2022 年冬奥会的圆满举行，冰雪运动蓬勃发展，冰雪产业加快壮大，河北在冬奥会筹办和本地发展两方面，都交上了优异的答卷。

一生只为绿山富民的"太行山上的新愚公"李保国，当代青年学生火热的青春绽放在西部大地上。燕赵儿女在向第二个百年奋斗目标进军的新征途上书写更加光辉灿烂的河北篇章。

第13章

百年奋斗

——开辟强省之路

　　河北是一块革命的土地、英雄的土地，是"新中国从这里走来"的土地。河北与新中国同频共振，取得了一个又一个成就，京畿大省崛起于渤海之滨。

　　1952年，河北省全省生产总值仅为40.5亿元，1978年达到183.1亿元，1991年、2005年、2010年分别实现了千亿元、万亿元、2万亿元的历史性突破，2021年超过4万亿元。

　　河北产业结构调整实现历史性转变，2018年第三产业跃升为河北省地区生产总值的首位。"十三五"时期，高新技术产业增加值年均增长11.2%，数字经济占河北省GDP比重超过30%。

张家口怀来县大数据基地

河北钢铁生产车间

京津冀协同发展、雄安新区规划建设、北京冬奥会筹办落地见效，重大国家战略和国家大事为河北发展带来宝贵历史机遇和强大势能。

河北的百年奋进历程，是中华民族从沉沦而奋起、由苦难到辉煌的缩影。

百余年前，民族困厄，苍生落难。

为"达到建立一个恢复民族自主、保护民众利益、发达国家产业之国家之目的……"，1927年，革命先驱李大钊（河北乐亭人），在他的遗作《狱中自述》中发出了最后的呐喊。

1949年，天安门城楼上，伴随着毛泽东同志的庄严宣告，新中国呱呱坠地，中华民族从此开辟了历史的新纪元。

然而，奇迹的起笔处，却是"满目萧条，百废待兴"的"一张白纸"。毛泽东同志曾感慨地说："现在我们能造什么？……一辆汽车、一架飞机、一辆坦克、一辆拖拉机都不能造。"

贫穷不是社会主义！没有钢铁就意味着没有高楼大厦、车船枪炮，更谈不上现代化建设和人民生活的富足。1957年，国家决定扩建和新建3个大型、5个中型、18个小型钢铁企业，邯钢是河北唯一上榜项目。此后，全省规划建设了多个钢铁厂。

凭借燕山、太行山两大山脉富集的铁矿资源，河北钢铁业骤然崛起。1972年，河北省开始成为工业大省，第二产业稳超第一产业。进入21世纪，河北省跃升为全国产钢第一大省，产量突破亿吨大关，相继超越德国、美国、日本。

然而，在历史性辉煌中，风险也加快聚集。2008年，受国际金融危机冲击和产能过剩等因素影响，钢铁行业的利润率呈断崖式下降。与此同时，能源消耗和环境污染日趋加重，钢铁大省转型迫在眉睫。

这一年，唐钢集团、邯钢集团组建河北钢铁集团，全省钢铁产业集中度大大提升。

2013 年，国家开始化解钢铁过剩产能。河北以行之有效的措施、壮士断腕的勇气、置之死地而后生的壮志，打响了去产能攻坚战。

坚决去，去发展新空间——突出钢铁、煤炭、水泥、平板玻璃、焦炭、火电六大行业，超额完成"十三五"时期去产能任务，其中钢铁产能由峰值的 3.2 亿吨压减到 2 亿吨以内，基本实现钢铁退城目标，分流安置职工 15.07 万人，安置率 100%。

主动调，调出发展新动能——工业设计点石成金，万企转型成效显著，重点培育 12 个省级主导产业和 107 个县域特色产业。保定生产的长城汽车，成为民族汽车业的标杆。唐山下线的动车组，斩获中国优秀工业设计奖金奖。

加快转，转出发展高质量——2019 年 10 月，首届中国国际数字经济博览会在石家庄正定举办。"十三五"时期，全省科技进步贡献率从 46% 提高到 60%，高新技术企业达到 9 400 家。2020 年，全省 PM2.5 平均浓度较 2013 年下降了 56.9%，人民群众享受到更多的蓝天白云。

经受住蜕变的阵痛，迎来了升华的喜悦。

"十三五"期间，河北省三次产业结构优化为 10.7∶37.6∶51.7，居民人均可支配收入从 18 118 元增加到 27 136 元，乳制品产量居全国第一，单位 GDP 能耗下降 21.26%，主要经济指标高于全国平均水平。各项事业取得历史性新进展、发生历史性新变化。

在百年未有之大变局叠加新冠肺炎疫情冲击下，河北彰显出强大发展韧性，产业间结构调整实现历史性突破，产业内结构调整同样蹄疾步稳。

第一产业实现由单一以种植业为主的传统农业，向多业共同发展的现代农业转变。第二产业主体地位增强，2020 年工业战略性新兴产业增加值增长 7.8%，快于规模以上工业 3.1 个百分点。现代服务业发展迅猛，对第三产业增长贡献率在 2018 年就达到 75.2%。

今日之河北，正以创新、协调、绿色、开放、共享的新发展理念为引领，推动实现由经济大省向经济强省的华丽转身。

第14章
山城崇礼
——一座因冬奥会而焕发生机的城市

2015 年 7 月 31 日，中国北京获得 2022 年第 24 届冬季奥林匹克运动会举办权。"申奥又赢了"的北京，携手张家口走向了世界前台。

与夏季奥运会不同，冬奥会对气候有着严苛的要求。风速、风力、气温、能见度都直接影响着运动员的发挥。为了达到相关比赛条件，国际奥委会在主办城市的选择上条件极为严苛。冬季奥运会比赛核心气象指标有两条，一是 2 月份平均气温低于 0℃，二是 2 月份降雪量大于 30 厘米。两项指标中，任何一项的可能性低于 75% 的城市，都没有申请冬奥会主办地的权利。翻阅历届冬奥会的举办地，这些城市基本上都处于北纬 40° 到北纬 70° 之间。而张家口崇礼正好位于北纬 41° "世界黄金滑雪带"上，其得天独厚的自然条件，恰恰又能满足承办冬奥会的需要。

2022 年 2 月 4 日北京冬奥会成功举办，小城崇礼也备受瞩目。

位于张家口市崇礼区的北京冬奥会张家口赛区承担着 2 个大项 6 个分项的比赛，是产生金牌最多的赛区。随着冬奥会赛程的推进，越来越多的运动员走进崇礼，越来越多的目光也投向这里。这里的变化完全超乎想象，生动展现了中国效率、中国活力、中国速度。

取名"崇尚礼仪"之意的河北省张家口市崇礼区，曾是中国的贫困地区之一，直到 2015 年底，官方统计的当地贫困发生率还高达 16.81%。

崇礼地处内蒙古高原与华北平原过渡地带上，在阴山山脉东段大马群山余脉和燕山余脉交接处，连绵的崇山峻岭和密林深谷，使来自西北方向的冷空气和东南方向的暖湿气流在这里受到地形的抬升，形成降水。同时，崇礼森林覆盖率高，空气中充足的水汽也有利于降水形成，而且优良的植被也易于积雪存储。崇礼境内 80% 为山地，地势起伏连绵，坡度陡缓适中，最低温度可达零下 40 摄氏度。"降雪早、积雪厚、存雪期长达150 天"——这些，曾一度被当地百姓认为是阻挡他们脱贫致富的不利条件，但在专家眼中，却成了崇礼发展的优势。

随着冬奥之风吹进大山，崇礼的发展也步入了快车道。冬奥会改变了崇礼的命运，使崇礼由一个山城小镇成长为一个奥运城市。通过冬奥会的筹办，崇礼的基础设施改善了，

张家口崇礼太子城冰雪小镇

生态环境更美了。

2019年，崇礼正式退出贫困县序列，彻底脱贫摘帽，也是那一年的12月30日，世界上首条时速350公里的智能高铁——京张高铁正式通车，河北张家口正式进入京津冀"一小时生活圈"，北京和崇礼之间原先三个多小时的车程缩短为50分钟，两地之间的时空距离更近了。

小城崇礼之变，不仅是中国冰雪运动跨越式发展的一个亮点，更是冬奥会带动区域发展、促使包括群众福祉等全方位进步的真实写照。

现在崇礼仅大型滑雪场就有7家，雪道有169条，15条高级雪道还通过了国际认证。随着滑雪爱好者的到来和滑雪产业的迅速发展，崇礼酒店、餐厅、雪具店……各种旅游配套机构如雨后春笋般出现，城市的基础设施、形象面貌也越来越好。

奥运因城市更精彩，城市因奥运更美好。毫无疑问，冬奥给崇礼带来了翻天覆地的变化，那么，冬奥会过后的崇礼又将如何？凭借便捷的交通、完善的配套、升级的雪场，冬奥会过后的崇礼将会吸引更多的人来看一看，并体验一下在"华北地区最理想的天然滑雪区域"滑雪是种什么样的感觉。

事实上，崇礼人也在不断地思考和行动。目前，崇礼每3个人之中就有一个人从事跟体育、滑雪相关的工作，4万多人直接或间接进入了冰雪产业和旅游行业，端上了"雪饭碗"。未来，崇礼将紧紧围绕奥运遗产的可持续利用，继续加快京张体育文化旅游带建设，大力发展以冬季滑雪、夏季户外活动为主导的体育休闲产业，在提升"雪国崇礼、户外天堂"城市品牌的知名度和美誉度上下功夫。

春回大地，万物润生。小城崇礼，未来更美……

曾经，一到冬天就困守雪城；如今，冰天雪地已是金山银山。

这里，就是塞外山城——崇礼。

第15章
保定学院西部支教团队
——绽放在西部的火热青春

2014年4月25日，习近平总书记给保定学院西部支教毕业生群体代表回信，对他们的选择和坚守、奋斗和奉献给予肯定，勉励青年人以他们为榜样，到基层和人民中去建功立业，让青春之花绽放在祖国最需要的地方，在实现中国梦的伟大实践中书写别样精彩的人生。

保定学院西部支教优秀群体是当代青年的杰出代表，他们的事迹在2014年初经报道后引起广泛关注。这个群体先后获得中央文明办"中国好人群体·敬业奉献好人集体"、光明日报社与央视"特别关注乡村教师支教团体"、河北省"三八"红旗集体、团中央"中国青年五四奖章集体"等荣誉称号。

保定学院校训——德业兼修 知行并重

铺开地图一寸寸找，侯朝茹终于在塔克拉玛干沙漠东南角看到一个小黑点：且末。远是真远，但天地开阔。

2000年3月30日，新疆且末二中在保定学院招聘教师的面试开始了。此时，西部大开发的战鼓刚刚擂响。且末二中时任校长段军在招聘宣讲会上介绍，该校初一年级7个班有6个还没有班主任，"那里的孩子需要你们！"很多人一下子被"击中"了：被需要的青春，才最宝贵。侯朝茹当即签约，她在日记里写下："到西部去！我愿驾驭青春驰骋在生命的原野上，任他风雨雷电。"父母不舍，和她冷战了一个月。直到出发前一刻，母亲才一把抱住她，痛哭失声。

2000年8月5日，15个意气风发的身影与"到西部教书去"的旗帜交相辉映，在母校师生的欢送声中登上西行列车。

"他们是带着户口离开的。"保定学院党委书记胡连利回忆，"当时，大学生志愿服务西部计划还未启动，去西部工作没有任何特殊优惠政策。"先行者的故事，成了校园里口口相传的话题。

荀轶娜的英语课开始了，嗓音喑哑低沉。学生们凝神静听，讲台上照例放着他们备好的热水、润喉片，还有一张小纸条："荀老师，又起风沙了，多喝水，小声讲。"

刚到且末二中3个月，荀轶娜突然在课堂上发不出声来。经诊断，声带受损，原因：天气干燥、用嗓过度。

一周18节课、带三个班上百名学生，荀轶娜总是忙不够。而且末的风沙，是她和同事们面对的最大考验。

且末是全国面积第二大的县，近四成土地被沙漠覆盖。年降水量不足20毫米，年均沙尘天气近200天。沙尘暴一起，天地混沌，一米外就看不清人影。

吃口拌面，沙子先进嘴；当浮尘满屋，得用湿毛巾捂口鼻；嘴唇裂、嗓子肿、流鼻血是常事……

他们明白了段军校长的话：不是没从各地招过老师，但一场风沙过后，总会"刮"走几个。可他们没有走，反而越发心疼这里的孩子。"我们的世界里除了学生还是学生。下班后一起交流教学体会，然后又埋头于教案和作业中。"李桂枝回忆。第一个学期，为提高讲课水平，她在繁重工作间隙听课50多节，笔记记了几大本。

侯朝茹一边把历史课讲得深入浅出，一边自学考取了国家二级心理咨询师资格证，为缺少关爱的孩子们开心理课、做心理咨询。学生们喜欢她那间"能讲秘密的办公室"，有什么烦心事，就去找侯老师细细说。

荀轶娜默默锁起了"静音休养"的医嘱，照常上讲台。"声带小结、声带不闭合"的病症反复发作，严重时，就戴上麦克、耳机，再不行，就板书……

2003年，他们在且末带出的第一批初中生毕业了。孩子们的中考成绩在全巴州首次名列前茅，且末教育"老末"的帽子摘掉了！

侯朝茹最大的幸福，是往日学生成了今天的同行。

2013 年，从新疆师范大学毕业的周文绯回到且末，当了一名教师，"我要和侯老师站在一起"。自掏腰包设奖学金、对生病学生悉心照顾……支教教师所付出的关爱俯拾皆是。

也有很多很多爱，向他们涌来——

那是刚到且末二中时，"校门前净水泼街、师生们列队欢迎"的淳朴热情；那是地震突袭时，伸向站在最后、组织撤离的老师的一双小手："您跟我们一起跑啊！"那是学生辗转 40 多公里背来的一袋土豆、家长专门做的烤包子、家里最大最甜的几个香梨……"爱出者爱返。"被他们汗水浸润的西部大地，也给了他们美好回报。事业上收获丰硕——他们大多成长为教学带头人、学校管理者，创造的教学方法多次在巴州、南木林等地各校推广。

父母越来越理解、支持。有的举家搬来一起生活，成为"边疆一家人"；有的满怀深情写来长信："孩子，不要再提'不孝'……你在边疆教书育人，给边疆栽上万朵鲜花，就是最大的孝！"

"我们选择了平凡，但没有平庸……我们愿意做一棵棵红柳、一株株格桑花，扎根西部、坚韧不拔、甘于吃苦、平实做人，为广袤的土地带去无尽的生命力！"在给习近平总书记的信中，他们这样写道。

截至 2021 年，保定学院已有 26 名毕业生自愿到西部工作、生活，他们把一腔赤诚和师者大爱献给边疆人民，把青春与梦想安放在西部大地。

第16章
人工天河跃峰渠
——太行山上的奇迹

　　新中国成立初期，紧靠漳河北岸的磁县西部和南部土地贫瘠，十年九旱，水源短缺，每年只能种植一季，粮食亩产不足200斤。面对如此局面，在邯郸专署的大力支持下，磁县县委决定劈开太行山，引进漳河水，以"重新安排河山"的雄心壮志改变当地贫穷落后的面貌。这一决定，使跃峰渠成为了漳河上游第一个开建的大型引水工程。

邯郸 跃峰渠

但随着新中国三年自然灾害的暴发，跃峰渠工程于 1960 年不得不暂停施工。这一年，同样引水自漳河的河南林县红旗渠宣布开工。时隔 6 年后，1966 年，跃峰渠重新开工，此后，经过了艰苦卓绝的奋战和大规模的改建、扩建和衬砌，直到 1977 年工程才全部结束。主干渠钻山跃岭，绕岗跨涧，引漳济滏，沿途穿过 28 座山峰，跨越 74 条沟壑，建渡槽、隧洞、涵洞、桥闸等较大建筑物 178 座，被世人誉为"人工天河"。

　　跃峰渠西起漳河小三峡，东至东武仕水库，主干渠全长 57.2 km，设计灌溉面积 35 万亩，年平均引水 1.0 亿立方米，至今已累计引水 63 亿立方米。涉及磁县 10 个乡镇、197 个自然村，29.5 万人因此受益。半个世纪以来，已经发展成以农业灌溉为主，集人畜饮水、防洪、发电、工业用水等多功能为一体的大型水利工程，为磁县的工农业生产和经济发展起到重要的支撑作用，也为邯郸市的工业用水和生态补水提供了重要的保障。

　　进入 21 世纪后，随着干旱天气的逐年加剧，跃峰渠又承担了新的任务。尤其是在 2009 年和 2010 年，磁县遭受多年不遇的严重干旱，降水量偏少，东武仕水库水位不断下降，库区渔业养殖和邯郸市工业用水需求一度陷入困难，东武仕水库急需引源补水。市、县两级政府发出了向东武仕水库应急调水的指示。关键时刻，当地政府果断采取措施，积极制定输水计划，两度从漳河向东武仕水库应急调水共计 2 928.01 万立方米，为邯郸市用水需求做出了重要贡献。

　　2016 年 7 月 19 日，磁县遭遇百年一遇的特大暴雨，致使磁县跃峰渠多处塌方、淤积，建筑物损毁，陷入瘫痪状态，大的地方有 21 处，大小加起来有 108 处，完全丧失了其所承担的引水、输水、灌溉、供水等功能。曾经美丽的"人工天河"满目疮痍……

　　面对灌区工程遭受前所未有的暴雨灾害，磁县跃峰渠全体干部职工不畏不惧，不等不靠，发扬"艰苦奋斗、自力更生"的跃峰精神，在县委县政府的坚强领导下，第一时间组织全体职工，重点在羊城段、辛庄隧洞、里青段、庆和峪段、驸马沟段等清理渠道淤积近 10 万平方米，疏浚渠道 20 余千米，临时修复主干渠 10 个节制闸、泄洪闸，恢复启闭功能。

　　如今，磁县跃峰渠早已恢复了往日的风采，部分渠段通水能力甚至超过"7·19"灾前水平，战天斗地的跃峰渠精神又注入了新的时代内涵，跃峰渠干部职工正与 50 万磁县干部群众一道谱写着新时代的水利建设之歌！

第 17 章

太行山上新愚公

—— 李保国科技扶贫

　　35 年如一日扎根太行山，他努力为群众脱贫寻觅出路，用科技把荒山秃岭抛进历史，把绿水青山留给未来；每年进山"务农"超过 200 天，他生前吃着馍就白开水当餐饭，用担当让贫穷困苦成为过去，让富裕文明渐成现实。他就是"人民楷模"、开创山区扶贫新路的太行山上"新愚公"——李保国。

　　1958 年，李保国出生于河北省衡水市武邑县的一个农村家庭。1981 年，作为恢复高考后的第一届大学生，李保国在河北林业专科学校（河北农业大学林学院前身）毕业后留校任教。上班仅十几天，他便和同事们一起扎进太行山，搞起了山区开发研究。

　　太行山区最不缺的就是大石头，最缺的就是土地。在河北省邢台市前南峪村（抗日战争时期，前南峪村是中国人民抗日军政大学总校所在地），看着一座座"石头山"，李保国来了"杠头"劲儿。他跑遍了山上的沟沟壑壑，认为爆破整地（爆破整地是一种

李保国科技馆

土地开发和整理方法，通过使用爆破技术来破碎土壤、岩石等地表物质，从而达到平整土地、改善土地条件的目的。这种方法通常用于地形复杂、土壤质地较硬的地区，以便于进行建筑开发、基础设施建设或农业耕作等。）在改善土质方面大有可为。土加厚了，水留住了，树木的成活率从原来的 10% 提高到 90%。在此基础上，李保国开始引导农民种板栗。几年下来，前南峪不仅成了远近闻名的富裕村，还成了"太行山最绿的地方"之一。

从前南峪村开始，李保国就把"家"安在了太行山区。为了帮助邢台市岗底村百姓致富，李保国潜心研究出 128 道苹果标准化生产管理工序。2015 年前后，仅苹果种植这一项，村民人均年收入就从不足百元达到 3 万多元。

岗底村党总支书记杨双牛回忆说："他真是为我们这些穷乡亲着想，心里就是想着老百姓。经常是起早贪黑，钻沟爬岭，越是刮风下雨越上山，研究他的课题。他自己这样做，他要求他的学生也这样做。老百姓看在眼里，疼在心里，人家是个大学教授，像这样为咱岗底村服务，从内心非常感激他。"

"是共产党员，我就要为人民服务；是教师，我就要为学生服务。"这是李保国的口头禅，也是他教学工作的真实写照。为了能让学生们更好做到理论与实践相结合，李保国把大批学生"赶"到田间地头去。他常说："搞科研就要像农民种地一样，春播秋收，脚踏实地。扎不进泥土地，就长不成栋梁材。"

如何把论文"写在"大地上？李保国妻子、河北农业大学林学院研究员郭素萍说："经济林专业，就是跟实践紧密结合的，保国通过往点上跑，一方面给农民带来很大效益，帮助农民走了一条脱贫致富的路，同时也不断补充教材、教学内容，使学生们也愿意听他的课。"

长期的科研工作、大量的科研成果、丰富的实践经验，李保国最了解学科的前沿、农村的需要、果农的期盼。他及时把自己的科研成果和在实践中获得的经验充实到教学内容中，把生产一线的信息及时更新在教材和授课中。

2016 年 4 月 10 日，李保国因心脏病突发，抢救无效，永远离开了他的家人、他的学生、他的太行山里的乡亲们⋯⋯30 多年间，李保国先后完成山区开发研究成果 28 项、技术推广及应用面积 1 826 万亩，让 140 万亩荒山披绿，带动山区农民增收 58.5 亿元。他淡泊名利，既不拿农民给的报酬，也不要企业的股份，终其一生保持了共产党人的清正廉洁、无私奉献。

李保国被追授"全国优秀共产党员""改革先锋""最美奋斗者""时代楷模""全国脱贫攻坚模范"等称号。2019 年，被授予"人民楷模"国家荣誉称号。

第18章
塞罕坝机械林场
——生态文明建设的中国样本

在河北省承德市北部、内蒙古浑善达克沙地南缘，有一片115万亩的人工林海，这里就是塞罕坝机械林场。从卫星云图上看，它犹如一只展翅的雄鹰，守卫着华北地区的生态安全。

很难想象，半个多世纪前这里是"黄沙遮天日、飞鸟无栖树"的荒僻苦寒之地。近60载寒来暑往，三代塞罕坝人牢记使命、艰苦创业、绿色发展，在极其恶劣的自然环境中，营造出世界上最大的人工林。

塞罕坝国家森林公园入口

塞罕坝是蒙汉合璧语，全称"塞堪达巴罕色钦"，意为"美丽的山岭水源之地"。历史上，塞罕坝曾是一处水草丰沛、森林茂密的天然名苑，是一片绿洲，是皇家猎苑。后来，开垦伐木使这里逐渐变成了一望无际的荒漠，黄沙荡荡，看不到尽头。

　　为了改变"风沙紧逼北京城"的严峻形势，新中国决定在河北北部建立大型机械林场。1962 年，来自全国 18 个省份的 127 名大中专毕业生奔赴塞罕坝，与当时林场的 242 名干部职工一起，肩负"为首都阻断沙源、为京津涵水源"的神圣使命，开始了战天斗地的创业史。

　　塞罕坝最低气温零下 43.3℃，年平均温度零下 1.3℃。林场第一批建设者赵振宇回忆说："当时到处是沙地和光山秃岭，风卷着沙粒雪粒遮天盖日，打到脸上像刀割一样疼。"

　　当时，没有任何住处可以挡风遮雨，生活条件极其艰苦。建设者住马棚、搭窝棚、挖地窖。一个窝铺住进 20 人，没有门板，就用草苫子代替，夜里戴着皮帽子睡觉都冻彻骨髓。早上起来，屋内到处是冰霜，褥子冻结在炕上。能吃着全麸黑莜面，就着咸菜，喝着雪水，就算是美味了。

　　生存条件极端恶劣，加之高寒高海拔地区造林经验更是几乎为零，1962、1963 年连续两年造林成活率不到 8%。一次又一次造林失败，动摇了人们的信心。关键时刻，时任林场党委书记王尚海等 4 位林场领导破釜沉舟，把家从外地搬到塞罕坝，很快稳定了军心。

　　1964 年春天，塞罕坝开展了提振士气的"马蹄坑大会战"。气温很低，建设者们浑身的泥浆冻成冰甲，走起路来咣咣直响，但没有一个人叫苦叫累，终于造林 516 亩，树木成活率达到 90% 以上。塞罕坝的造林事业从此开足马力，也由每年春季造林发展到春秋两季造林，最多时每天造林超过 2 000 亩，一年造林达到 8 万亩。

　　如今，塞罕坝第一代创业者们已至暮年，他们用理想和信念、用青春和热血铸就了"绿色丰碑"，所凝结的"塞罕坝精神"也跨越时空薪火相传。

　　1973 年到坝上的第二代创业者邓宝珠说，选择林业，就是选择奉献，他的两个儿子如今都在林场，从事林场护林员和施工员工作。

　　1980 年出生的于士涛是河北保定人，大学刚毕业就一头扎进塞罕坝。"干林业的都默默无闻，因为你做的事情，40 年以后才能看到结果。"他说，"我们将紧握前辈们的接力棒继续奋力前行。"

　　2008 年，刘军和妻子王娟来到林场中海拔为 1 900 米的月亮山"望海楼"当瞭望员。当年，"望海楼"不通水电暖，大雪封山时半年无人迹。每到重要防火期，刘军夫妇每隔 15 分钟就要瞭望辖区方圆 20 公里林海的火情并汇报。"像对待自己的孩子一样对待每一棵树"，是夫妻俩的工作态度。

　　创业难，守业更难。这片绿来之不易，守护好这片绿也并非易事。一点火星、片刻大意，都可能让这片林海毁于一旦。

　　为确保森林资源安全，现在的塞罕坝林场建立了"天空地"一体化森林防火预警监测体系，实现了卫星、无人机、探火雷达、视频监控、高山瞭望、地面巡护有机结合，

塞罕坝七星湖秋色

快速反应。

自 1962 年以来，一代代塞罕坝人听从党的召唤，用心血、汗水和生命创造了荒漠变绿洲的绿色奇迹，生动诠释了"革命理想高于天"的坚定信念，以及忠于党和人民事业的使命担当。

据中国林科院评估，塞罕坝百万亩林海筑起了一道牢固的绿色屏障，有效阻滞了浑善达克沙地南侵，每年为滦河、辽河下游地区涵养水源、净化淡水 2.84 亿立方米，防止土壤流失量为 513.55 万吨；每年可固定二氧化碳 86.03 万吨，释放氧气 59.84 万吨。

塞罕坝良好的生态环境和丰富的物种资源，使其成为珍贵、天然的物种基因库，现有陆生野生脊椎动物 261 种、鱼类 32 种、昆虫 660 种、大型真菌 179 种、植物 625 种。塞罕坝也因此成为"生态文明建设范例"，生动诠释了"绿水青山就是金山银山"，被联合国环境规划署授予"地球卫士奖"。

如今的塞罕坝，自然风光辽阔壮美，历史内涵深邃厚重，满蒙民俗风情独特，有着丰富、秀美的生态旅游资源，被誉为"河的源头、云的故乡、花的世界、林的海洋"，已经成为华北特别是环京津地区最著名的生态旅游景区之一。

第4篇

人杰地灵　河北大地多才俊

河北省作为中华民族的发祥地之一，物华天宝，人杰地灵；燕赵文化源远流长，博大精深；在漫长的历史岁月中，涌现出许多著名的历史人物，他们推动影响着历史的进程，丰富着历史的内涵，成为河北的标志及形象代言人。

这里，涌现了赵武灵王、荆轲、荀子、董仲舒等千古传颂的代表人物，他们不仅将锐意改革、重信尚义、忧国忧民的正气和责任感深深地烙刻在燕赵大地上，也塑造和影响了整个中华民族的精神气质和价值取向。

这里，书写过中国文学史上不朽的"邺下风流"，也记录过盛唐边塞诗的慷慨雄浑，还孕育培养了一大批著名元曲作家，并见证着他们走向元曲创作巅峰。

第19章
诗词歌曲

1. 古文诗学的流传及"毛诗"

　　《诗经》是中国最早的一部诗歌总集，在文学史上拥有极高的地位。这部典籍经秦始皇"焚书坑儒"，传承几近断绝。汉武帝"罢黜百家，独尊儒术"时，《诗经》的传授仅有齐人辕固、鲁人申培、燕人韩婴和赵人毛苌四家，分别被称为"齐诗""鲁诗""韩诗"和"毛诗"。其中齐、鲁、韩三家为今文诗学，侧重于以诗喻时，魏晋以后逐渐衰亡。"毛诗"为古文诗学，侧重于古义古训。东汉时，马融著《毛诗诂训》，郑玄为之笺注，毛诗盛行，南宋以后传下来的只有"毛诗"一家。其所承载的原旨要义，对后人研习《诗经》具有重要价值，为中国乃至世界诗歌文学做出了重要贡献。相传，孔子删定《诗经》后，经子夏、曾申、孟仲子、根牟子、荀子、毛亨（俗称"大毛公"）传给毛苌（俗称"小毛公"）。毛苌早年流落于河间郡崇德里（今属沧州市），到汉景帝时，河间献王刘德修学好古，在河间城北设立"君子馆"招徕文人贤士，毛苌应聘，随命开馆讲学，传授《诗经》。毛苌传授《诗经》和寓居之处，即现在河间市古洋河畔的"诗经村"。后人为纪念他，在村旁修建了他的衣冠冢及毛公祠堂、毛公书院。

2. 宫廷音乐家李延年

　　李延年，西汉中山（今保定定州）人，是汉武帝时期的著名乐官。"倾城倾国"成语最早来源于他演唱的《北方有佳人》："北方有佳人，绝世而独立。一顾倾人城，再顾倾人国。宁不知倾城与倾国，佳人难再得。"这是迄今留存最早的五言诗雏形，在诗歌发展史上有着启发后人的意义。

3. 汉乐府诗及《陌上桑》

　　"乐府"是从汉武帝开始设置的管理音乐事务的官署，也负责民间采风，并将搜集的各地歌谣配以乐曲。乐府诗主要收录在《汉书·艺文志》和宋代郭茂倩编著的《乐府诗集》之中，其中有多首诗歌从内容上可考证出发生在邯郸、沧州河间等地。如《汉书·艺文志》收录的《鸡鸣》《相逢行》，《乐府诗集》收录的《陌上桑》等，尤其是《陌上桑》堪称名篇，是一首艺术性极高的五言叙事诗，与后来出现的《木兰辞》《孔雀东南飞》齐名，其中名句几乎妇孺皆知、代代传诵。崔豹的《古今注》认为它是从邯郸的一个生活故事演变而来，是对当时这类故事的概括和升华。

4. "建安风骨"及邺下文人集团

东汉末年，建安年间乃至魏晋初期，战乱频仍、社会动荡、百姓罹难，但也是文坛上"俊才云蒸"，文学空前繁盛和辉煌的时代。这一时期所形成的文学被文学史家盛赞为"建安文学"或"建安风骨"，其特点是发扬汉代乐府民歌的现实主义精神，以反映人民疾苦、追求建功立业为主要内容，诗歌风格慷慨悲凉、语言刚健爽朗，尤其是普遍采用新兴的五言形式，把五言诗发展到一个高峰，对中国诗产生了极其深远的影响。其中代表性人物有曹操、曹植、曹丕，合称"三曹"，孔融、陈琳、王粲、徐干、阮瑀、应场、刘桢被称为"建安七子"。当时，曹氏父子在汉代魏郡治所邺城（今邯郸市临漳县）

毛亨

营建邺都，筑金凤、铜雀、冰井三台，且雅好文学、招揽文士，让他们聚集在此开展文学及政治活动，因此被后世称为邺下文人集团。

5. 高适和他的边塞诗

唐初至盛唐，四方征讨，边关战事频仍，形成了盛唐诗坛著名的边塞诗派。其兼容建安风骨和绮丽的齐梁笔致，呈现出慷慨壮丽的风格，洋溢着昂扬的时代精神，不仅有一定的思想意义、认知价值，而且具有很高的审美情趣。在大批边塞诗人中，渤海蓚（今衡水景县）人高适是最负盛名的诗人之一，与岑参并称"高岑"。其素有雄图大志，一生两度出塞，去过辽阳、河西，对边塞生活有深刻体会。诗作常常结合壮丽的边地景色，表现驰骋沙场、建立功勋的英雄壮志，抒发慷慨从戎、抗敌御侮的爱国情怀，反映征人思妇的幽怨和士卒们的牺牲、艰苦。《塞下曲》《燕歌行》堪称唐代边塞诗的代表作。

第 20 章

元曲杂剧

元朝时期，由于民族矛盾、社会问题、城市经济畸形发展、通俗文化需求等因素，特别是知识分子地位居于九流之末，混迹于市井，介入杂剧创作，使得元曲以其开阔的思想内容、完善的艺术形式风行于世，成为与唐诗、宋词、汉文章相媲美的艺术奇葩，在灿烂的中国文学及戏剧发展史上独树一帜。当时的河北地区是京畿之地，涌现了关汉卿、白朴、马致远、王实甫四位有"元曲四大家"之称的泰斗级人物，以及尚仲贤、李好古、纪君祥、王和卿、杨果、刘秉忠、卢挚、珠帘秀、鲜于必仁等，他们从事元曲创作，同时有的还直接参加演出，使得河北的元杂剧创作与演出在中国文化及戏剧发展史上称雄一代。

关汉卿为元代大都蒲阴（今保定安国）人，伟大的戏剧家，被誉为中国古代戏剧的奠基人，1958 年被列入世界文化名人。所作杂剧 60 余种，现存 13 种，散曲现存小令 57 首、套曲 13 首、残曲 4 首，为元曲四大家之首，作品对当时及后世影响极大。他本人擅长歌舞，精通音律。代表作有《窦娥冤》《单刀会》《望江亭》《救风尘》《蝴蝶梦》等，至今仍是许多剧种的保留剧目，尤其一出《窦娥冤》"地也，你不分好歹何为地？天也，你错勘贤愚枉做天！"的愤怒质问，感天动地、令人回味无穷。

白朴是元代真定（今石家庄正定）人，生于南宋末年，遭逢丧乱，自幼随元好问长大，聪慧过人，博览群书，通史书经传，尤深钻律赋之学。一生共写了 16 个杂剧，现存散曲 4 个套曲、37 首小令，另有词集《天籁集》。有的咏唱男女恋情，有的感叹人生无常，有的描写自然景色。其作品文辞工整，清隽秀美，俊逸有神；特别是那些咏唱恋情之作，词义浅显，却不轻佻，不庸俗，富于民歌色彩，颇得后世好评。流传下来最出色的代表作有《裴少俊墙头马上》《唐明皇秋夜梧桐雨》，前者是中国十大古典喜剧之一，后者讲的是唐玄宗与杨贵妃的故事，曲词语言华美绮丽，开元杂剧"文采派"先河。

马致远为元代广平（今邯郸永年）人，有杂剧 15 种，今存 7 种，小令和套曲 120 余首。代表作《汉宫秋》是中国十大古典悲剧之一，写王昭君出塞的故事。清人评价："写景写情，当行出色，元曲中第一义也。"他的越调《天净沙·秋思》"枯藤老树昏鸦，小桥流水人家，古道西风瘦马。夕阳西下，断肠人在天涯"，是元散曲典范之作，被称为"千古秋思之祖"。

王实甫是元代易州定兴（今保定定兴）人，有杂剧14种，今存全本3种、残本2种。代表作《西厢记》是至今最为流传的大型元杂剧，影响深远、妇孺皆知。其中"愿天下有情的都成了眷属"一声咏唱，振聋发聩、荡气回肠，大胆冲击了千年封建礼教，数百年来不知博得多少人的喜爱。元末明初戏剧评论家贾仲明称誉："西厢记天下夺魁。"曹雪芹《红楼梦》里评价说："词句警人，余香满口。"

河北梆子戏《窦娥冤》

尚仲贤是元代真定（今石家庄正定）人，作杂剧11种，今存3种，残篇断曲数种，代表作《柳毅传书》。他擅长刻画人物的情态和个性特点，语言鲜活，如该剧第一折："往常时凌波相助，则我这翠鬟高插水晶梳。到如今衣衫褴褛，容颜焦枯。不学他萧史台边乘凤客，却做了武陵溪畔牧羊奴。思往日、忆当初，成缱绻、效欢娱。他鹰指爪、蟒蛇躯，忒躁暴、太粗疏。但言语，更喧呼，这琴瑟怎和睦。可曾有半点儿雨云期，敢只是一划的雷霆怒。我也不恋你荣华富贵，情愿受鳏寡孤独。"鲜明地表现出一个娇生惯养的龙宫少女牧羊时的凄戚感情，人物情态跃然纸上，不愧为元曲能手。

李好古为元代保定（今保定市）人。作杂剧3种：《巨灵神劈华岳》《赵太祖镇凶宅》《张生煮海》，皆为神话剧，今存《张生煮海》。明代朱权《太和正音谱》评其词"如孤松挂月，清秀优美，磊落不凡"。元末明初贾仲明《凌波仙·吊李好古》云："芳名纸上百年图，锦绣胸中万卷书，标题尘外三生簿。《镇凶宅》赵太祖，《劈华山》用功夫，《煮全海》张生故。撰文李好古，暮景桑榆。"

纪君祥是元代大都（今北京）人，作品有杂剧6种，现存《赵氏孤儿》为中国十大古典悲剧之一，国内外多种剧种均有演出。另存《陈文图悟道松阴梦》残曲一折。

王和卿是元代大名（今属邯郸）人，陶宗仪《南村辍耕录》说他滑稽佻达，传播四方。与关汉卿相友善，尝讥谑汉卿。现存散曲小令21首、套曲1首，见于《太平乐府》《阳春白雪》《词林摘艳》。作品有醇厚的俗谣俚曲色彩和俳优习气，笔调辛辣、滑稽嘲谑、借以讽世，以辛辣、滑稽、嘲谑的口吻来讥讽这个世界。

第21章
散文杂记

1. 中华辞赋之祖荀况及先秦散文的最高阶段

    战国时赵国人荀况是杰出的思想家、文学家，先秦诸子中最后一位大师。文学方面，他不仅是与孟子齐名的散文大师，后世史家将其与屈原并列为中华辞赋之祖。所著《荀子》32篇，总结和发展了先秦哲学观点，在当时的"百家争鸣"中独树一帜。其文学思想重质尚用，反对华而不实。《劝学》篇里"青取之于蓝，而青于蓝；冰水为之，而寒于水"，成为千古传诵的名句。《赋篇》包括《礼》《知》《云》《蚕》《箴》五篇，是一种散文式的赋体。"辞赋"一词即取屈原《楚辞》和荀子《赋篇》各一字相合而成。汉代著名文学家、历史学家班固评论："大儒孙卿及楚臣屈原，离谗忧国，皆作赋以风，咸有恻隐古诗之义。"（《汉书·艺文志》）可见荀子在中国文学发展史上的地位。其中《成相》篇是伴着乐器演唱的民谣式通俗文学作品，因此有学者还把荀子视为中华弹词之祖。

《水经注》三峡篇

2. "别开生面"的著作《水经注》

北魏范阳涿县（今保定涿州）人郦道元对魏晋时代无名氏所著《水经》一书作注释写成《水经注》。这是一部"别开生面"的著作，作者历览群书，博采汉魏以来文献所载山川景物、风土人情、神话传说、历史掌故，并结合自己随魏文帝巡幸长城、阴山，以及自己在各地做官时"访渎搜渠"的实地调查，以简洁优美的文字，叙述了 1 200 多条河流的发源地点、流经地区、支渠分布、古来河道的变迁。书中描摹出祖国锦绣河山的风貌，表现了作者的爱国思想和对人民的同情。《水经注》不仅是一部杰出的地理典籍，而且文字幽丽峭洁，描写深细，不同山水，各具个性，是一部引人入胜的山水游记散文著作。

3. 堪称骈体文范本的历史文献《洛阳伽蓝记》

南北朝时期北平（今保定满城）人杨衒之所著《洛阳伽蓝记》是一部颇具文学价值的历史文献。文笔俏丽，骈中有散，颇具特色。北魏时期，京城洛阳曾兴建佛寺千余所，木衣锦绣，极尽奢华，后经战乱，多毁于兵火。东魏孝静帝武定五年（547 年），杨衒之重过洛阳，见城廓崩毁，宫室倾覆，寺观灰烬，庙塔丘墟，恐后世无闻，作《洛阳伽蓝记》（分城内及四门之外共五篇），记述佛寺园林的盛衰兴废。作品以佛寺盛衰为纲目，杂以园林、人事、掌故，内容丰富，夹叙夹议，叙事多用散文，描写常用骈俪。既可列为重要的地理、历史著作，又堪称难得的优秀散文作品，因此被后世誉为魏晋南北朝时期骈体文的范本。其中尤以《法云寺》《寿丘里》等节最著名。

4. 享有"千古奇文"之誉的《吊古战场文》

唐朝赞皇（今属石家庄）人李华是著名古文家、古文运动的先驱之一，在开元天宝年间与兰陵萧颖士齐名，有所谓"古称管鲍，今则萧李，有过必规，无文不讲"的称誉。在李华一生所写的大量记、序、传、论之中，《吊古战场文》堪称千古奇文。作品先以景物描写作铺垫，继以丰富的想象表现了戍卒戍边、临阵厮杀、三军覆没的惨烈场面，然后宕开一笔回顾了自战国至汉代战乱频仍的历史，最后写了阵亡者家眷"哭望天涯"的祭奠，并发出"时耶命耶？从古如斯"的慨叹。韵散参半，情挚语哀，气势雄浑，惨恻动人，后人多模仿，却难以企及。

第22章
古代小说传奇

1. 丰富多彩的民间神话传说

　　神话传说是先民们口头创作出的最早的文学形式，是孕育华夏文学的根基和土壤，对后世文学产生了深远影响。华夏民族具有标志性的神话传说几乎都源自河北或与河北有着渊源：盘古开天地源自沧州青县，那里遗存有盘古祠；女娲娘娘炼石补天、抟土造人源自太行山南麓，邯郸涉县遗存有娲皇宫；伏羲创八卦源自石家庄，新乐遗存有伏羲台；保定流传有黄帝元妃嫘祖采桑养蚕的传说；张家口涿鹿流传有"黄帝战蚩尤"的故事；保定顺平、邢台隆尧流传有尧帝实行禅让制、创"尧天舜日"盛世的故事；衡水流传有大禹治水、划分九州的故事；等等。

清康熙年间所制五彩仙人乘槎图盘

2. 中国早期笔记体小说代表作

西晋范阳方城（今廊坊固安）人张华所著之《博物志》，是仿《山海经》体而演变的志怪小说。原有 400 卷，晋武帝嫌其冗杂，命删减至 10 卷，以记述异境奇物、琐闻杂事为主，掺有一些神仙道术之事，为中国早期笔记体代表作。在中国文化史上，虽比不上所谓名门正派的经史之书，但毕竟是对中华民族古代文化的一种保存，是中国文化有机体的一个组成部分。对研究中国古代思想、神话、文化和历史都很有资料价值，特别是其中关于我国西北地区石油和天然气的记载，颇有参考意义。其中《薛谭学讴》《乘槎》等篇较为优秀，为后人称扬。

3. 广为流传的《中山狼传》

明朝故城（今属衡水市）人马中锡的寓言体小说《中山狼传》是我国文学史上的名篇，塑造了"东郭先生"和"狼"这两个典型的艺术形象。描写战国时赵简子行猎中山，有一条狼被追逐甚急，适遇东郭先生，乞求庇护，得以脱险；危机一过便露出凶恶的本相，恩将仇报，想吃掉东郭先生。作品在极力刻画狼的凶险阴狠、忘恩负义的同时，塑造了东郭先生这迂腐懦弱、滥施仁慈的人物形象，是一篇文德具存的佳作，问世不久，即被改编为杂剧上演。至今仍在群众中流传，颇有教育意义。

4. 伟大的古典名著《红楼梦》

我国四大古典名著之一《红楼梦》（原名《石头记》），成书于清代乾隆年间，一般认为作者曹雪芹祖居唐山丰润。作品通过对封建家族兴衰历程的艺术升华，对当时社会生活深刻、细腻、全方位的描写，对封建礼教、统治思想、科举制度、包办婚姻等进行了深刻的批判，但也反映出作者为封建制度"补天"的幻想和找不到出路的悲观情绪。整部作品规模宏大，结构谨严，语言优美生动，善于刻画人物，塑造了许多富有典型性格的艺术形象，具有高度的思想性和卓越的艺术成就，是古代长篇小说中现实主义的高峰。其思想艺术力量，不但震动了当时社会，还引起后人持续不断的研究热情，从而产生了"红学"研究。

Appendix
附 录

河北省全国重点文物保护单位名录

1. 河北省全国重点文物保护单位名录（近现代重要史迹及代表性建筑）

序号	名称	年代	地址
1	冉庄地道战遗址	1942 年	保定市清苑区
2	西柏坡中共中央旧址	1948 年	石家庄市平山县
3	李大钊故居	1889 年	唐山市乐亭县
4	晋察冀边区政府及军区司令部旧址	1938 ～ 1948 年	保定市阜平县
5	八路军一二九师司令部旧址	1940 年	邯郸市涉县
6	山海关八国联军营盘旧址	清	秦皇岛市山海关区
7	北戴河近代建筑群	清至民国	秦皇岛市北戴河区
8	丰润中学校旧址	1913 ～ 1925 年	唐山市丰润区
9	义和拳议事厅旧址	1898 年	邢台市威县
10	育德中学旧址	1907 ～ 1937 年	保定市莲池区
11	保定陆军军官学校旧址	1912 ～ 1923 年	保定市莲池区
12	察哈尔都统署旧址	1914 ～ 1928 年	张家口市桥西区
13	布里留法工艺学校旧址	1917 ～ 1919 年	保定市高阳县
14	晏阳初旧居	1926 ～ 1936 年	定州市
15	潘家峪惨案遗址	1941 年	唐山市丰润区
16	中共晋冀鲁豫中央局和军区旧址	1946 ～ 1948 年	邯郸市武安市
17	唐山大地震遗址	1976 年	唐山市路南区

（续表）

序号	名称	年代	地址
18	马厂炮台	清	沧州市青县
19	开滦唐山矿早期工业遗存	清	唐山市路南区
20	滦河铁桥	清	唐山市滦州市
21	察哈尔民主政府旧址	清至民国	张家口市宣化区
22	直隶审判厅旧址	清至民国	保定市莲池区
23	秦皇岛港口近代建筑群	清至民国	秦皇岛市海港区
24	光园	民国	保定市莲池区
25	正丰矿工业建筑群	民国	石家庄市井陉矿区
26	大名天主堂	1921 年	邯郸市大名县
27	耀华玻璃厂旧址	1922 年	秦皇岛市海港区
28	光明戏院	1934 年	沧州市河间市
29	晋冀鲁豫边区政府旧址	1942 ～ 1945 年	邯郸市涉县
30	晋察冀军区司令部旧址	1945 ～ 1946 年	张家口市桥东区
31	中国人民银行总行旧址	1948 年	石家庄市新华区
32	左权将军墓	1950 年	邯郸市邯山区

2. 河北省全国重点文物保护单位名录（石窟寺及石刻）

序号	名称	年代	地址
1	响堂山石窟	东魏、北齐至元	邯郸市峰峰矿区
2	义慈惠石柱	北齐	保定市定兴县
3	赵州陀罗尼经幢	北宋	石家庄市赵县
4	龙兴观道德经幢	唐	保定市易县
5	天护陀罗尼经幢	唐	石家庄市井陉矿区
6	大观圣作之碑	宋	石家庄市赵县
7	大唐清河郡王纪功载政之颂碑	唐	石家庄市正定县
8	五礼记碑	唐至宋	邯郸市大名县

（续表）

序号	名称	年代	地址
9	宋璟碑	唐	邢台市沙河市
10	大佛顶尊胜陀罗尼经幢	金	秦皇岛市卢龙县
11	朱山石刻	汉、唐	邯郸市永年区
12	封龙山石窟	南北朝至明	石家庄市元氏县
13	水浴寺石窟	南北朝至明	邯郸市峰峰矿区
14	八会寺刻经	隋	保定市曲阳县
15	邢台道德经幢	唐	邢台市襄都区
16	卧佛寺摩崖造像	北宋	保定市唐县
17	法华洞石窟	宋至清	邯郸市武安市
18	瑜伽山摩崖造像	宋、明	石家庄市平山县
19	木兰围场御制碑、摩崖石刻	清	承德市围场满族蒙古族自治县、隆化县
20	狄仁杰祠堂碑	唐	邯郸市大名县
21	曲里千佛洞石窟	明	邯郸市涉县

3. 河北省全国重点文物保护单位名录（古遗址）

序号	名称	年代	地址
1	赵邯郸故城	战国	邯郸市邯山区
2	燕下都遗址	战国	保定市易县、定兴县
3	磁山遗址	新石器时代	邯郸市武安市
4	中山古城遗址	战国	石家庄市平山县
5	邺城遗址	曹魏至北齐	邯郸市临漳县
6	涧磁村定窑遗址	唐至元	保定市曲阳县
7	许家窑——侯家窑遗址	旧石器时代	张家口市阳原县
8	北戴河秦行宫遗址	秦	秦皇岛市北戴河区
9	磁州窑遗址	北齐、隋、宋、元	邯郸市峰峰矿区、磁县

（续表）

序号	名称	年代	地址
10	邢窑遗址	隋至五代	邢台市内丘县、临城县
11	泥河湾遗址群	旧石器时代	张家口市阳原县
12	南庄头遗址	新石器时代	保定市徐水区
13	西寨遗址	新石器时代	唐山市迁西县
14	代王城遗址	春秋至汉	张家口市蔚县
15	井陉窑遗址	隋至清	石家庄市井陉县
16	元中都遗址	元	张家口市张北县
17	金界壕遗址	金	承德市丰宁满族自治县
18	爪村遗址	旧石器时代	唐山市迁安市
19	石北口遗址	新石器时代	邯郸市永年区
20	北福地遗址	新石器时代	保定市易县
21	钓鱼台遗址	新石器时代	保定市曲阳县
22	台西遗址	商	石家庄市藁城市
23	东先贤遗址	商	邢台市信都区
24	南阳遗址	周	雄安新区容城县
25	讲武城遗址	战国至汉	邯郸市磁县
26	常山郡故城	汉	石家庄市元氏县
27	土城子城址	南北朝	张家口市尚义县
28	边关地道遗址	宋	廊坊市永清县
29	会州城	辽至明	承德市平泉市
30	刘伶醉烧锅遗址	金至元	保定市徐水区
31	九连城城址	金至元	张家口市沽源县
32	海丰镇遗址	金	沧州市黄骅市
33	小宏城遗址	元	张家口市沽源县
34	大名府故城	宋	邯郸市大名县
35	四方洞遗址	旧石器时代	承德市鹰手营子矿区
36	化子洞遗址	旧石器时代	承德市平泉市

（续表）

序号	名称	年代	地址
37	孟家泉遗址	旧石器时代	唐山市玉田县
38	筛子绫罗遗址	新石器时代	张家口市蔚县
39	三各庄遗址	新石器时代	雄安新区雄县
40	哑叭庄遗址	新石器时代至东周	沧州市任丘市
41	万军山遗址	新石器时代、商	唐山市迁安市
42	庄窠遗址	新石器时代、商	张家口市蔚县
43	三关遗址	新石器时代、商、战国	张家口市蔚县
44	南城村遗址	新石器时代、商、汉	邯郸市冀南新区
45	涧沟遗址	新石器时代、商、汉	邯郸市复兴区
46	补要村遗址	新石器时代、商、唐	邢台市临城县
47	顶子城遗址	夏至周	承德市平泉市
48	龟地遗址	夏至周	唐山市丰润区
49	北放水遗址	夏、东周、汉	保定市唐县
50	要庄遗址	商至周	保定市满城区
51	伏羲台遗址	商、周、汉	石家庄市新乐市
52	西张村遗址	西周	石家庄市元氏县
53	柏人城遗址	西周至东周	邢台市隆尧县
54	鹿城岗城址	东周	邢台市信都区
55	固镇古城遗址	东周至东汉	邯郸市武安市
56	付将沟遗址	战国至汉	承德市兴隆县
57	东垣古城遗址	战国至汉	石家庄市长安区
58	武垣城址	战国至汉、隋唐	沧州市肃宁县
59	东黑山遗址	战国、汉	保定市徐水区
60	古宋城址	汉	石家庄市赵县
61	冀州古城遗址	汉	衡水市冀州区
62	后底阁遗址	北朝至唐	邢台市南宫市
63	临清古城遗址	北魏至金	邢台市临西县

序号	名称	年代	地址
64	隆化土城子城址	北魏至元	承德市隆化县
65	禅果寺遗址	南北朝	邯郸市武安市
66	沧州旧城	唐至宋	沧州市沧县
67	板厂峪窑址群遗址	明	秦皇岛市海港区
68	郛堤城遗址	战国、秦汉	沧州市黄骅市
69	贝州故城遗址	宋	邢台市清河县
70	太子城遗址	金	张家口崇礼区
71	西土城遗址	金	张家口市康保县

4. 河北省全国重点文物保护单位名录（古墓葬）

序号	名称	年代	地址
1	封氏墓群	北魏至北齐	衡水市景县
2	清东陵	清	唐山市遵化市
3	清西陵	清	保定市易县
4	中山靖王墓	汉	保定市满城区
5	磁县北朝墓群	南北朝	邯郸市磁县
6	献县汉墓群	汉	沧州市献县
7	下八里墓群	辽	张家口市宣化区
8	赵王陵	战国	邯郸市丛台区、永年区
9	汉中山王墓	汉	定州市
10	逯家庄壁画墓	东汉	衡水市安平县
11	北齐高氏墓群	北朝至隋	衡水市景县
12	梳妆楼元墓	元	张家口市沽源县
13	邢国墓地	周	邢台市信都区
14	所药村壁画墓	汉	保定市望都县
15	隆尧唐祖陵	唐	邢台市隆尧县

（续表）

序号	名称	年代	地址
16	张柔墓	元	保定市满城区
17	怡贤亲王墓	清	保定市涞水县
18	纪晓岚墓地	清	沧州市沧县
19	林村墓群	战国至汉	邯郸市复兴区
20	无极甄氏墓群	东汉至北朝	石家庄市无极县
21	赞皇李氏墓群	南北朝	石家庄市赞皇县
22	宋祖陵	五代、宋	保定市清苑区
23	王处直墓	五代	保定市曲阳县
24	石羊石虎墓群	辽至金	承德市平泉市
25	杨赟家族墓地	元至清	张家口市蔚县
26	北张庄墓群	汉	邯郸市邯山区

5. 河北省全国重点文物保护单位名录（古建筑）

序号	名称	年代	地址
1	娲皇宫及石刻	北齐、明、清	邯郸市涉县
2	定县开元寺塔（料敌塔）	北宋	定州市
3	开福寺舍利塔	北宋	衡水市景县
4	普利寺塔	北宋	邢台市临城县
5	武安舍利塔	北宋	邯郸市武安市
6	长城	春秋至明	保定市等
7	大运河	春秋至清	廊坊市等
8	张家口堡	汉、魏晋南北朝、唐、明、清	张家口市桥西区
9	沧州铁狮子	后周	沧州市沧县
10	永通桥（小石桥）	金	石家庄市赵县
11	广惠寺华塔	金	石家庄市正定县

序号	名称	年代	地址
12	临济寺澄灵塔	金	石家庄市正定县
13	源影寺塔	金	秦皇岛市昌黎县
14	成汤庙山门	金	邯郸市涉县
15	开化寺塔	金至明	石家庄市元氏县
16	双塔庵双塔	金至明	保定市易县
17	皇甫寺塔	金至明	保定市涞水县
18	古莲花池	金至清	保定市莲池区
19	澍鹫寺塔	金至元	张家口市阳原县
20	玉泉寺大殿	金至元	邯郸市涉县
21	隆兴寺	宋	石家庄市正定县
22	宝云塔	宋	衡水市桃城区
23	修德寺塔	宋	保定市曲阳县
24	庆林寺塔	宋	衡水市故城县
25	静志寺塔基地宫	宋	定州市
26	净众院塔基地宫	宋	定州市
27	安济桥（大石桥）	隋	石家庄市赵县
28	治平寺石塔	唐	石家庄市赞皇县
29	幽居寺塔	唐	石家庄市灵寿县
30	解村兴国寺塔	唐	保定市博野县
31	南贾乡石塔	唐	邢台市信都区
32	开元寺	唐至清	石家庄市正定县
33	凌霄塔	唐至宋	石家庄市正定县
34	正定文庙大成殿	五代	石家庄市正定县
35	万寿寺塔林	五代至清	石家庄市平山县
36	北岳庙	元	保定市曲阳县
37	慈云阁	元	保定市定兴县
38	柏林寺塔	元	石家庄市赵县

（续表）

序号	名称	年代	地址
39	正定府文庙	元	石家庄市正定县
40	半截塔	元	承德市围场满族蒙古族自治县
41	金山寺舍利塔	元	保定市涞水县
42	天宁寺前殿	元	邢台市襄都区
43	常乐龙王庙正殿	元	邯郸市涉县
44	释迦寺	元、明	张家口市蔚县
45	平乡文庙大成殿	元至明	邢台市平乡县
46	金河寺悬空庵塔群	元至明	张家口市蔚县
47	定州清真寺	元至清	定州市
48	九江圣母庙	元至清	邯郸市武安市
49	阁院寺	辽	保定市涞源县
50	开善寺	辽	保定市高碑店市
51	涿州双塔	辽	保定市涿州市
52	南安寺塔	辽	张家口市蔚县
53	庆化寺花塔	辽	保定市涞水县
54	天宫寺塔	辽	唐山市丰润区
55	圣塔院塔	辽	保定市易县
56	西岗塔	辽	保定市涞水县
57	兴文塔	辽	保定市涞源县
58	佛真猞猁迤逻尼塔	辽	张家口市宣化区
59	大辛阁石塔	辽	廊坊市永清县
60	永安寺塔	辽	保定市涿州市
61	伍侯塔	辽	保定市顺平县
62	涞水龙严寺塔	辽	保定市涞水县
63	万里长城——山海关	明	秦皇岛市山海关区
64	金山岭长城	明	承德市滦平县

（续表）

序号	名称	年代	地址
65	宣化古城	明	张家口市宣化区
66	蔚州玉皇阁	明	张家口市蔚县
67	万里长城——紫荆关	明	保定市易县
68	毗卢寺	明	石家庄市新华区
69	万里长城——九门口	明	秦皇岛市海港区
70	昭化寺	明	张家口市怀安县
71	鸡鸣驿城	明	张家口市怀来县
72	泊头清真寺	明	沧州市泊头市
73	暖泉华严寺	明	张家口市蔚县
74	真武庙	明	张家口市蔚县
75	常平仓	明	张家口市蔚县
76	蔚州灵岩寺	明	张家口市蔚县
77	单桥	明	沧州市献县
78	弘济桥	明	邯郸市永年区
79	永年城	明	邯郸市永年区
80	纸坊玉皇阁	明	邯郸市峰峰矿区
81	大道观玉皇殿	明	定州市
82	邢台开元寺	明	邢台市襄都区
83	伍仁桥	明	保定市安国市
84	万全右卫城	明	张家口市万全区
85	洗马林玉皇阁	明	张家口市万全区
86	灵寿石牌坊	明	石家庄市灵寿县
87	蔚县关帝庙	明	张家口市蔚县
88	天齐庙	明	张家口市蔚县
89	蔚州古城墙	明	张家口市蔚县
90	故城寺	明	张家口市蔚县
91	重光塔	明	张家口市赤城县

（续表）

序号	名称	年代	地址
92	永平府城墙	明	秦皇岛市卢龙县
93	下胡良桥	明	保定市涿州市
94	普彤塔	明	邢台市南宫市
95	滏阳河西八闸	明	邯郸市经济技术开发区
96	天青寺大殿	明	邯郸市武安市
97	保定钟楼	明	保定市莲池区
98	正定城墙	明	石家庄市正定县
99	邢台清风楼	明	邢台市襄都区
100	正定梁氏宗祠	明	石家庄市正定县
101	药王庙	明、清	保定市安国市
102	涉县清泉寺	明清	邯郸市涉县
103	寿峰寺	明至民国	唐山市丰润区
104	井陉古驿道	明至清	石家庄市井陉县
105	扁鹊庙	明至清	邢台市内丘县
106	永济桥	明至清	保定市涿州市
107	西古堡	明至清	张家口市蔚县
108	福庆寺	明至清	石家庄市井陉县
109	时恩寺	明至清	张家口市宣化区
110	宣化柏林寺	明至清	张家口市宣化区
111	卜北堡玉泉寺	明至清	张家口市蔚县
112	方顺桥	明至清	保定市满城区
113	登瀛桥	明至清	沧州市沧县
114	洗马林城墙	明至清	张家口市万全区
115	黄粱梦吕仙祠	明至清	邯郸市丛台区
116	井陉旧城城墙	明至清	石家庄市井陉县
117	沙子坡老君观	明至清	张家口市蔚县
118	蔚县重泰寺	明至清	张家口市蔚县

（续表）

序号	名称	年代	地址
119	聚馆古贡枣园	明至清	沧州市黄骅市
120	普宁寺	清	承德市双桥区
121	普乐寺	清	承德市双桥区
122	普陀宗乘之庙	清	承德市双桥区
123	须弥福寿之庙	清	承德市双桥区
124	避暑山庄	清	承德市双桥区
125	直隶总督署	清	保定市莲池区
126	殊像寺	清	承德市双桥区
127	安远庙	清	承德市双桥区
128	定州贡院	清	定州市
129	溥仁寺	清	承德市双桥区
130	腰山王氏庄园	清	保定市顺平县
131	金门闸	清	保定市涿州市
132	大慈阁	清	保定市莲池区
133	承德城隍庙	清	承德市双桥区
134	普佑寺	清	承德市双桥区
135	净觉寺	清	唐山市玉田县
136	定州文庙	清	定州市
137	衡水安济桥	清	衡水市桃城区
138	凤山关帝庙	清	承德市丰宁满族自治县
139	淮军公所	清	保定市莲池区
140	清河道署	清	保定市莲池区
141	深州盈亿义仓	清	衡水市深州市

References

参考文献

［1］陈正祥. 中国历史文化地理 [M]. 太原：山西人民出版社，2021.

［2］胡克夫. 燕赵文化丛书 [M]. 石家庄：河北教育出版社，2016.

［3］黄仁宇. 中国大历史 [M]. 北京：生活·读书·新知三联书店，2021.

［4］康金莉. 大运河河北段历史文化记忆 [M]. 北京：北京师范大学出版社，2021.

［5］梁思成. 中国建筑史 [M]. 北京：生活·读书·新知三联书店，2011.

［6］桑献凯，曹征平，王宁. 大河之北 [M]. 石家庄：花山文艺出版社，2021.

［7］王智. 燕赵传奇 [M]. 石家庄：河北教育出版社，2015.

［8］许倬云. 中国文化的精神 [M]. 北京：九州出版社，2021.

［9］郑绍宗. 河北古长城 [M]. 石家庄：河北教育出版社，2016.